"*Becoming His Bride* is a timely book, as many are looking to Jesus for hope in a world marked by isolation and loneliness. Many want intimacy with Jesus, but struggle to feel divine connection. Karen, in her transparent and humble manner, has given us hope and tools for how we can hear his voice and experience his close presence. She has a personal relationship with Jesus that compels the reader to want the same.

I was captivated by each journal entry where God's familiar written Word was infused alongside His more personal words to Karen. I found myself reaching for my journal and listening intently for what the Lord might want to say to me. She awakened in me a desire to listen more in prayer, journal more of His words, and rest in just being with Him. Some of the most gripping parts of her story were the prayers God gave her for others during her own trial: her children, her pastor, and her church.

This is a book that not only tells of hope in Christ, but shows us how to access it with practical methods. It is an important book for people who are looking for authentic interaction with God in daily life. It is also a must-read and great encouragement for those touched by suicide. I will be passing it to my grown daughters!"

—**Cindy Woodford,** *Former Bible Study Fellowship Teaching Leader, Knoxville, Tennessee*

"Karen begins her book with one of the hardest, most shocking things that can happen to a person. She goes on to show how God has drawn her close, and how she was and is called to turn to the Beloved in times of grief and in times of joy. She relates how she was given direction and strength—not only to get through this challenging time and sustain her children—but to flourish and share her experience with others.

As Karen's childhood neighbor, I have known her my whole life. This book demonstrates her surrender to the lessons God has given her and helps me see more clearly how she survived her experiences. Her obedience and faithfulness have led her to be the strong, caring woman she is now. She is showing us how she was carried by the Lord so that we may be as well."

Jana Ostrom, BS, MS, *Clinical Pharmacist (Retired),*
Seattle, Washington

This is a perfect book to read for a hurting heart. Karen Wiley leads her readers along a journey of desperation, to find healing through the power of prayer. A must read for anyone needing encouragement and guidance.

Dianne Taylor, RN, *Pastor's Wife of 40 Years*

Becoming
His Bride

Becoming
His Bride

Finding Intimacy with Jesus

KAREN LUNDE WILEY

Karen Lunde Wiley

Isaiah 54:5

Inspira

To order additional books:
www.amazon.com
www.karenlundewiley.com

E-book also available.
ISBN: 978-1-7332679-8-4

Editorial and Book Packaging: Inspira Literary Solutions, Gig Harbor, WA
Book Design: PerfecType, Nashville, TN
Cover Design: Brianna Showalter
Illustration: Julia Alyssa Oddonetto
Printed in the USA by Ingram Spark

The Lord reached down from on high and took hold of me;
he drew me out of deep waters.
He rescued me from my powerful enemy,
from my foes, who were too strong for me.
—Psalm 18:16

Table of Contents

TABLE OF CONTENTS

Acknowledgments

It was God who taught me about the importance of prayer, but He used my mother—who was an amazing example—to show us how prayer could be a powerful and essential part of our lives. My mother helped start a prayer group at her church when I was a toddler. When I was 18—and a brand-new believer—I often attended that very same prayer group with my mom. Even after growing up, getting married, and moving to Tennessee, I would spend Tuesday mornings with my mom and her prayer partners every time I came home to visit. For over fifty years, my mother's prayer group was a constant in the lives of many. My mom went to be with Jesus in 2012, but she left an incredible legacy and her example impacted my personal prayer life forever.

My sisters, Kathy and Kay, have supported me in prayer since they put their faith in Jesus so many years ago. They were both part of my prayer team and their faith prayed this book into existence. They have prayed for me, my writing, and this project every step of the way, along with some dear friends: Twinkle, Sue T., and Sharon.

Friends from Bible Study Fellowship have also been a part of this team: Diane H., Lynn, Kim, and Denise. My small group of twenty years has supported me in prayer all of these years and now, in the writing of this book. Thank you: Amy, Gail, Karen F., Sandra, Sue H., and Susan L. I could not have done this without all of you. I know there are others who have prayed silently in their homes when God has placed it on their hearts, and to you I am just as grateful.

Thank you to my editors and writing coaches, Arlyn Lawrence and Heather Sipes, who reside in Gig Harbor, Washington where my mom grew up! Knowing that God chose them specifically for this job, along with their team, gave me such peace.

To my adult children, who experienced much of this journey as young teenagers: It wasn't easy, but we have grown and changed in many ways, together. I am so thankful for both of you and love you beyond what words could ever express.

To my new husband, hand-picked and chosen by God to be a very important part of this latest journey in my life. On top of being my loving husband, he is also my typist, editor, researcher, encourager, and manager of all business details. I love you, Michael Rae Young!

And last but most important, I give *all* credit in the writing of this book to my Father God Who created me, Jesus Christ Who saved me, and the Holy Spirit Who breathed every word in this book into me. I am honored to have been the vessel, but ALL glory goes to my Triune God! Hallelujah!

Foreword

Long before Karen Wiley became an author, she was learning how to give authentic voice to the deepest layers of her heart. First in journals, then with friends and family, then with groups and gatherings, Karen opened her heart as a powerful testimony to the heart of her God. *Becoming His Bride* now widens the circle of people who engage God's love through the heart of Karen's story.

I have spent a good bit of time looking more deeply at the painting which Karen offers as her opening to her narrative. Filled with bold colors and brilliant light, the imagery is layered with joyous hope. My eyes are immediately, and continuously, drawn toward the blinding presence of the Groom awaiting the bride. As I considered Karen's story and the vision she has painted with her words, I was reminded of the Apostle Paul's glorious declaration of hope in Romans 5:2-5:

> *Through him we have also obtained access by faith into this grace in which we stand, and we rejoice in hope of the glory of God. Not only that, but we rejoice in our sufferings, knowing that suffering produces endurance, and endurance produces character, and character produces hope, and hope does not put us to shame, because God's love has been*

poured into our hearts through the Holy Spirit who has been given to us.

Karen's journey, narrated by her journal entries, urges all of us toward that Hope. She risks significant vulnerability in the process, inviting the reader to do so as well. In fact, I think this is the power of *Becoming His Bride*. In the painting, the bride is adorned for the wedding. She is beautiful and hopeful. Yet, if you look closer, she is vulnerable in that moment. Only Hope in the Groom draws her forward. Only He can provide the Strength, the Courage, and the Grace to stay on the journey. And only His love makes the journey worth the struggle.

Ultimately, it is Christ's love in Karen's heart, found equally present in tragedy as well as triumph, that compels us toward Him. As we take each vulnerable step forward, His Holy Spirit confirms that we are securely His Bride, even in the often messy process of becoming His bride. Karen tells that story powerfully, authentically, simply because it is her story of becoming.

Karen invited me into her story as her way of sharing His Story with me. I am so thankful that you've been invited into His Story as well. The Groom awaits you as you lift one foot in front of the other by His Power.

Entrusted by Grace,
Rick Dunn
Lead Pastor, Fellowship Church
Co-host, LIFE REFRAMED Podcast

There is a time for everything, and a season for every activity under the heavens: a time to weep and a time to laugh, a time to mourn and a time to dance . . .
(Ecclesiastes 3:1,4)

The seasons of life are all part of God's plan. My process of becoming God's bride included these seasons as well—many of them very uncomfortable.

As I described the vision of *Becoming His Bride* to my niece, Julia Alyssa, I asked her if she could include the seasons in her painting. Her portrayal of the vision God gave me was so perfect that when I saw it, it brought me to tears.

In this painting, the bride is presently on the path in the spring. Spring represents a time of new life and new beginnings. This happens first, at the time of salvation. Then, she skips into summer—a time of deep love, joy, and laughter. Next, she climbs up the path to fall, struggling with questions and uncertainties. The path grows steeper and steeper, until winter is filled with heartache and tragedy. Out of darkness comes the light, and she returns to spring with greater wisdom and a lighthearted spirit, and the cycle begins all over again.

Can you find yourself in this painting? What season are you facing right now? As you read this book, I pray it will lead you to new ways of connecting with your heavenly bridegroom, regardless of your present season.

Thank you, Julia, for your incredible creativity and execution of this beautiful painting.

To see the painting in full color, visit:
www.karenlundewiley.com

Introduction

In Him we were also chosen, having been predestined
according to the plan of Him who works out everything
in conformity with the purpose of His will.
                                                    —Ephesians 1:11

"All new life comes out of the dark places."
                                                    —Ann Voskamp

The chapters in this book are an intimate retelling of an incredible period of my life—a journey that has lasted a lifetime. Within these chapters are two love stories—one involving the first love of my life, my late husband, David, and one involving my Father God, the King of my Heart and my Great Redeemer. Woven between the pieces of my story, you will find letters from my King—words I have received from God as He drew me closer to Him in the years following my late husband's death. This book captures the events and the essence of those first, early years of learning to walk through life with Jesus as my Bridegroom.

You see, my story is one of great sadness, but also one of great, redeeming love. My hope is that through these stories and letters, readers will be able to see how Scripture and intimacy with Jesus brought me through one of the darkest events imaginable. My God made beauty from ashes—utter, all-encompassing heartbreak. Despite the deepest, darkest shadows of grief and chaos, I came to know that I am chosen in love and predestined by grace.

What I didn't acknowledge at the time was that—at the same time He was teaching me, Karen, how to live as His beloved—I sensed He was also giving me a message He would one day ask me to share with you. That message is that ALL of us are His beloved. Together, we all are the Bride of Christ—His church. And that is the message I hope you come away with from this book: YOU too are His beloved. You are predestined, cherished, provided for, protected, and valued more than you can ever know.

Here I sit, more than two decades after The Event. My children have grown up and moved away. My siblings live nearly 3,000 miles away. Sometimes I have cried out, "Why, Lord? Why would all of this be in Your great plan? Why did you choose me?" Although I felt at times as if I were drowning in my sorrow, God has always pulled me out of the waters. We are on a journey together that has not only healed and strengthened me personally, but that has also allowed many others to know the beauty and love of our Father God.

In this book, my hope is that you will see past my pain to His plan, and our perfect dance of divine love. He's asking you to dance, too.

*M y plan will unfold before you like a
rosebud bursting into bloom,
watered by the raindrops of My Holy Spirit and
warmed by the rays of My precious Son, Jesus Christ.
Your life is My life in you.*

The Day that Changed
Everything

I t was August of 1994.

My family—which consisted of fourteen-year-old Andrea, eleven-year-old Josh, my husband David, and myself—was completely overwhelmed. Some of it was fairly typical family stress. Andrea was struggling under the weight of her responsibilities as dance team captain, daily dance classes after school, and cross-country training. Josh was adjusting to a new middle school and was taking karate classes. I was returning to teaching first grade after taking the summer off, and so I was adjusting again to my new school schedule as well as the responsibilities of being a full-time mom. My husband, however, may have been under the most stress of all.

After teaching history at a local middle school for nineteen years, David had chosen to move to high school for a change of pace. Change was always difficult for him—it made him anxious and overwhelmed. As he was the "new kid on the block," so to speak, he had been assigned a classroom down in the basement, one with no windows. This in and of itself was a challenge to him, as David was a marathon runner, a biker, and a hiker. He craved—no, he needed—fresh air. His new classroom was dark and dank and had an abundance of mold. In no time, David was waking up with cold-like symptoms and intense chest congestion. This was quite an experience for him, because he never got sick!

David's newfound anxiety from all the change, combined with his sickness, caused him to stop sleeping. Sleeping is hard enough for teachers during the first weeks back to school, but this time was different. David was completely unable to sleep for seven straight days. Although we didn't know it at the time, the burdens he was fighting at the time were too much for him to handle on his own. He was fighting a physical battle, but also a spiritual one.

On the morning of August 24th, I returned from my early morning run and was stretching on our front porch when I heard what I thought was a huge limb hitting the roof of our house. I looked around but could see nothing. There was not even a sliver of wind moving the air. After a few seconds, I realized it was a gun shot. I ran inside to find my husband moaning in our bed. Before I even finished dialing 9-1-1 . . . he was gone. David had committed suicide.

Almost immediately, a thick darkness moved in and consumed me. I went through the motions of notifying the right people—David's sister, Mary, our pastor and his wife, and the schools at which we worked. Somehow, family and friends were notified as well, though I don't remember calling them.

I'll never forget the sound of my teenage daughter sobbing in the shower that morning. To this day, it was the last time I heard her cry. I'll never forget the look on my young son's face as he turned his face toward the ambulance that was taking his father's body away. "Mom," he said. "I'm not mad at God."

Me. . . well, I couldn't cry. My eyes would leak tears from time to time, but not a sound came from me for days on end.

The very next day, I had to go and pick out a casket. I was hardly in the room with the sales representative for more than five minutes before I had to run out so I wouldn't get sick. I stood outside to get some fresh air and attempted to collect myself. I could not go back in. *God . . . how will I ever get through this?*

That night I had a dream. I dreamed I got up in front of the entire congregation at David's funeral and spoke. When I woke up, though I felt instantaneous dread, I felt sure I had been given a sign from God. I sensed He had a message He wanted to share not only to me, but through me. It went like this:

Do not be downcast. Do not be disturbed, for your hope is in Me. I am your Light in the darkness. I am your Joy in the midst of your pain. I am Rest for your weariness. I am the Song on your lips. I am the One who will carry your heavy load, if only you will release it to Me. I am your companion and your Friend, so you need not be lonely. I am your All in All. Look to Me. I am always in your presence. Are you in Mine?

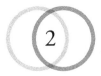

First Days without David

Before I knew it, it was Friday afternoon and we were driving in a van to Central Baptist Church for a reception with friends, and then the funeral. When we got there, I stood for over two hours with my two children flanking me, shaking the hands of every person present. As I touched their hands with my own, I could feel God speaking to me. *He believes,* I'd hear Him whisper, or, *She believes,* or, *He doesn't believe.* Deep down, I knew. I knew! It was clear to me that I needed to speak, and God had something to say to each person who was present in that room. The receiving line was so long, the funeral director had to cut it short by passing out pages of the guestbook.

It's a fuzzy memory, punctuated with small moments of vivid recollection, but I remember being led down the aisle and seated in one of the front pews. As our pastor was speaking, I felt God nudge me. *Go!* He said. The last thing I wanted to do was go up there in front of so many people! But then, I felt it again. *Go!* Before I knew it, I was being carried up the stairs and toward the podium. Of course, I was not physically being carried, but it felt as if I had an angel on either side of me, doing the hard work of putting one foot in front of the other and supporting all of my weight and grief.

I stood there, looking at the more than 1,000 people who had gathered to honor David's life. As I spoke, I was carried once again. Without any effort, the words poured forth. I still don't even remember what I said, but I know that God did the hard work for me.

The days and weeks after losing David felt like the longest, shortest time. Every minute felt like it dragged on forever, but at the same time, it felt like each day was over before I had an opportunity to even process what had happened.

My mom stayed with the kids and me until Labor Day. All too quickly, it was time for the kids to return to school and before I knew it . . . it was my turn. However, I was carried once again, and I was filled with God's peaceful presence. His joy consumed me. People were amazed at the smile that remained on my face, but miraculously, I felt strengthened to comfort others instead of only dwelling on myself. I poured my life into my children and did everything within my power to keep our family afloat.

I spent every morning with the Lord. He showed me how deeply He cared for me and how much He loved me. How did I find delight in Him? I pursued Him. I read His love letter to me, the Bible. I immersed myself in His Word and our relationship.

My Precious One,
Be filled with my joy—joy in your pain and tribulation. These are a part of life, the life I have given to you. Live each day to the fullest. Live it as if it were your last. Feel My presence wherever you are and know that I am near. Know that as you seek Me, I am guiding you and directing the path that you are taking. I have ordained the pain you have experienced, and your life will bring glory to MY name. All is perfect for you. Trust Me completely and you will be filled with joy.

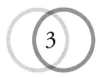

Rebuilding

He wakens me morning by morning,
wakens my ear to listen like one being taught.
—Isaiah 50:4b

By the summer of 1995, I realized it was time to make some changes, as life was never going to be the same. We spent that next summer with my family in Seattle. During this time, I attended summer school to learn how to teach dyslexic students. My kids seemed to enjoy their time with cousins and other extended family members. The time with them was good for everyone. But, the sweet, warm, Pacific Northwest summer came to an end, and it was time to return to Tennessee. At this, I became totally overwhelmed.

As the kids got back into school, they seemed to be adjusting well. I took this as an opportunity to focus on myself. Even though I was a seasoned teacher, I was nervous about getting back into teaching. And of course, there were all of the home responsibilities that I had essentially been ignoring for a year. The sympathy cards had stopped flowing. The offers for meals had stopped. As impossible as it seemed, I needed to figure out how to make my life (and myself) feel as "normal" as possible.

Sometimes, bitterness and anger toward David would seep into my soul. "You loved me! You loved your kids! How could you do this to us? How could you leave us like this?" Miraculously, God would find me in my anger and grief. As I fell to my knees, He would answer me.

I decided to help with a new church start-up in our area. This was a catalyst toward my healing—I poured my heart and soul into it. Whatever they asked me to do, I did it. As a way of coping and holding on to God, I made this church my mission. I began to teach a Sunday School class for adults. This is how I met my friend, Sue.

One Sunday, while I was teaching, Sue received a word from God that she was going to be my friend. Sue's immediate reaction was, *Uh, no thanks!*

To anyone on the outside, Sue and I were complete opposites. Because of my hidden insecurities, I had every hair in place, a pressed outfit, and high heels. Sue had wild, curly hair and wore a mini skirt. However, God drew her back to my class time and again.

Eventually, she fully surrendered to what God was impressing on her and showed up on my doorstep on a day I was laying on my couch, sick. If she really knew me, she would never have come. I hated people to see me whenever I felt less than "perfect." But she was listening to God and she was obedient. When she came into my living room, she noticed a journal laying on my coffee table. She picked it up and read it. It happened to be the words God had spoken to me that very morning.

She looked at me and said, "Where are the rest?"

I looked at her and said, "The rest? What do you mean?"

She said, "I know this isn't the first time you've written like this. Where are the rest of your journals?"

I shrugged my shoulders. "I threw them away," I told her.

"Why?" she asked earnestly.

I suddenly felt very exposed. "I get a message from Him every day . . . so I didn't think I needed to keep them," I said quietly.

She looked at me sternly and spoke as if the words were coming from God Himself. "Don't ever throw them away again!"

After that, I stopped journaling for a long time.

God had sent Sue to help me. I had a long list of jobs that needed my attention but with the responsibility of teaching school and caring for my children, the list never shortened—until Sue came. One of the first things she did for me was clean out David's closet. It was a painful, daunting task that I just couldn't face on my own. It hung over me like a heavy, black cloud.

One day, while I was at school, Sue went to my house, packed up his clothes, and took most of them to the Salvation Army. She also cooked dinner for us, so we had a hot meal when we got home. That day, she lifted a huge burden off of my shoulders.

Sue slowly whittled away at my list until everything was checked off. I went from feeling like I was drowning, to treading water, to actually making progress. Our friendship grew as we worked side-by-side on projects and attended church together. As trust was built, she shared her testimony with me. We had a lot to share and teach one another.

In time, I learned that in 1994, Sue had tried to kill herself. With her insight, I was able to learn a lot about the circumstances around David's death. God gifted her with an amazing ability to encourage me to talk, share, and grieve—all necessary steps to my healing. I believe it helped her to heal as well. God gave us this verse:

> *Two are better than one, because they have*
> *a good return for their work:*
> *If one falls down, his friend can help him up.*
> *But pity the man who falls and has no one to help him up!*
> *—Ecclesiastes 4:9-10*

My friendship with Sue was a God-given gift. God knew what I needed to survive, and He provided a way beyond my wildest imagination.

Getting to Know My
Heavenly Bridegroom

For where your treasure is, there your heart will be also.
—Matthew 6:21

In February, I finally got back to my journaling. On February 17, 1996, God called me back to Himself:

My Precious One,
I long to commune with you. I long to spend quiet time with you. Why do you ask, "Where are all of the people?" when you, too, fail to draw apart and spend intimate time with Me? Our time together should be top priority, and yet you allow the busyness of the world to steal our time. The lack of people at the prayer meeting was also a sign of the priorities of My people. If you could see all things, you would never rise from a praying position. You are in a spiritual battle that can only be won on your knees.

At some point, I'm not sure when, I heard God call me His "Precious One." It seemed to be the key to starting my writing. I would draw apart, pour my broken heart out to God, turn to paper, and write "My Precious One." It was kind of like turning on a faucet. The twist of the wrist and writing those words would start His words flowing from my thoughts onto the paper in front of me. . .

My Precious One,
Perseverance is a constant battle and a continual process. Day by day, you must rise up and go on. No matter what lies ahead or what has gone on behind, you must persevere. I am your Father God. I will provide for you all that you need to persevere. Depend on Me. Depend on My strength to carry you through.

Do not become overwhelmed by looking at the whole. Take one day at a time. Take one task at a time. Pray for back up and look to see the kind of help that I send you, and receive it as a gift from Me. Do not look at what is left undone and bemoan the fact.

Know that if you give your all to Me, all will be accomplished in My perfect timing and you need not worry or fret. You must learn to rely totally and completely on Me, resting in My presence in all places.

Joy. Joy in Me for the day of the Lord is at hand! I will provide for you all that you need. Do you trust Me? Do you believe it? Take captive all thoughts. Believe with your whole heart, mind, body, and soul. Let your faith be evident in all that you do.

Speak positively. Let your speech reflect your faith. Learn to continually rest in Me. Belabor nothing. My strength is yours to have. Draw from it. Use it and go on. Persevere and rejoice in all things.

I say" rejoice," for the day of the Lord is coming like a thief in the night. You must make yourself ready and be prepared.. Live your life to the fullest. Do all that I call you to do and do it with joy. Your attitude is a reflection of the depth of your faith and many are watching you to see how you respond.

Do not concern yourself with what many see in you, but instead be concerned about how I see you. Are you ready to face a new day of challenges? Are you ready to speak My truth and reveal My ways through your actions and reactions?

Be firm but be loving. Reflect Me, your Savior, in all that you do and say. Today is the day the Lord has made; rejoice and be glad in it forever. Amen.

———

My Precious One,
All is in My hands and the coming of My Kingdom is drawing near. Seek to use every opportunity for furthering the truths of My Kingdom. I will give you the words to speak if you will listen and seek to use them.

Look into My face. Hear Me speak and walk in obedience to My calling. I will provide you opportunities in rapid succession. The closer you are to Me and the more time you spend with Me, the more will multiply the opportunities you have to witness for Me.

In so many ways you are depleted. The course I have placed you on has made you weary and tired. You must be rejuvenated. Your joy must be made full again. By drawing apart with Me and seeking communion with Me and Me alone, your joy will be made full and your strength will be regained. Walk with Me. Talk with Me. Draw ever so near to Me. Never leave Me. Be aware of My constant presence, for it is never I who chooses to leave you!

———

"Why, you do not even know what will happen tomorrow. What is your life? You are a mist that appears for a little while and then vanishes."
—James 4:14

Struggles at Home

In 1994, it was David's death that knocked me down. But two years later, in 1996, I found myself being knocked down in a different way: navigating single parenting. More specifically, I struggled with my daughter and her behavioral reaction to intense, overwhelming grief. As far as I knew, Andrea had not shed a single tear since the day her dad died.

Josh, on the other hand, was more expressive. Shortly after David's death, he had the opportunity to go camping with another family. In the safety of these dear friends, he was able to express his deep emotions in outward ways. As time went on, he continued to vent his sorrow and anger, almost putting his fist through a door at one point! I believe the fact that he could express his feelings physically contributed to his ability to process them more quickly.

Andrea, on the other hand, held everything in. This was her way of trying to protect her brother and me. She felt she needed to "suck it up," and be strong for us all. But it was killing her on the inside. She tried to "move on"—which meant she delayed the inevitable processing of her grief and anger—and this ultimately exploded two years later. Now I found myself with a daughter who "ran away." Physically, she was still home, but she built a thick, impenetrable wall around herself. Even in her silence, her body was shouting, *Don't get too close! Don't touch me! Don't comfort me! Leave me alone!*

The week before Andrea's sixteenth birthday, I got a speeding ticket while trying to get us all to school on time. In the past, I had sworn that no child of mine would ever get a car at a young age. But now I found myself needing to eat my words. With my teaching schedule and the kids' school and their busy activity schedules, I needed her to be able to drive the two of them to school. It was just another thing I could not handle.

Within the week, Andrea had made a list of used cars she thought she'd like. We found ourselves driving away from a dealership a couple days later with one of the exact cars on Andrea's list that we'd found at an amazing price. It was a miracle! Then . . . the trouble began.

Having a car introduced all kinds of freedoms for Andrea and all sorts of new challenges for me. It brought me to my knees time and again.

My Precious One,
Have no anxiety about anything, but by prayer and supplication, with thanksgiving, let your requests be known to God and the peace of God that passes all understanding will keep your

heart and mind in Christ Jesus. Trust Me! Put your cares in My care. Andrea is My child. I love her deeply. I will protect her. All that occurs in her life will be for My glory. She has deep hurt and deep pain but I will heal her. Let us work these things out together. TRUST ME. ◎

I prayed and asked God to give me a verse for my Andrea. I closed my eyes and randomly opened up my Bible. Psalm 40:3 jumped off the page:

> *He put a new song in (her) mouth, a hymn of*
> *praise to our God. Many will see and fear*
> *and put their trust in the Lord.*

On that same day, God spoke this to me:

My Precious One,
I have heard your prayer and I have answered, for Andrea will have a new song. She will sing My praises and lives will be touched because of her witness. Her heart will be filled with My joy and there will be a song on her lips. Be patient, my child, for I am at work. I have much to do to accomplish My perfect plan. Just be a willing servant, ready to take up your cross and follow Me. It is the only way. Trust Me! ◎

I have been given Psalm 40:3 a dozen times over the years. Whenever I needed confirmation that God was holding my daughter in the palm of His hand—always during difficult circumstances—when I would cry out to Him, my Bible would literally fall open to this verse. To God be the glory!

One day I wrote in my journal:

> *My daughter and I had a real battle yesterday. We just don't see eye to eye. Lord, I just pray for truth to be revealed. I pray for her eyes to be opened, for the veil to fall—for her to come to repentance, Lord, so she can be the bold and godly woman you created her to be.*
>
> *Give me strength Lord, to sustain me through this battle. Help me stand tall and see the enemy at work, rather than my daughter. Release her soon, Lord, but only soon enough that she can receive the full blessing of this time.*
>
> *Give us both strength Lord, and do not let either one of us produce any irreparable damage upon one another, I pray.*

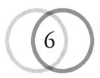

Fighting Spiritual Battles

Because of David's death and the circumstances surrounding it, I was becoming more and more aware of the spiritual battles we were all facing. I prayed fervently for protection—that God would place a hedge of protection around our entire household. I did not want to let the enemy get another foothold in our home! I read the scripture about our "spiritual armor," which talks about how God provides us with the tools we need to fight this spiritual battle:

> *Finally, be strong in the Lord and in his mighty power.*
> *Put on the full armor of God so you can take your stand*
> *against the devil's schemes.*
> *For our struggle is not against flesh and blood,*
> *but against the rulers, against the authorities,*
> *against the powers of this dark world*
> *and against the spiritual forces of evil in the heavenly realms.*
> *Therefore put on the full armor of God,*

so that when the day of evil comes,
you may be able to stand your ground,
and after you have done everything, to stand.
Stand firm then, with the belt of truth
buckled around your waist,
with the breastplate of righteousness in place,
and with your feet fitted with the readiness
that comes from the gospel of peace.
In addition to all this,
take up the shield of faith
with which you can extinguish
all the flaming arrows of the evil one.
Take the helmet of salvation
and the sword of the Spirit
which is the word of God.
And pray in the Spirit on all occasions
with all kinds of prayers and requests.
With this in mind, be alert
and always keep on praying
for all the saints.
—Ephesians 6:12-18

When my children were little, we would always finish getting dressed in the morning by figuratively putting on the Armor. One day, the Lord spoke to me and told me that it was not a child's game. He told me not to get out of bed and not to let my feet touch the ground before I put His armor on through prayer.

By praying for protection, I acknowledged my trust in God to care for my every need, physical and spiritual. It gave me confidence to face every situation during my day. And, as I navigated these difficult waters with my daughter, I knew that God was going to protect us and keep her safe.

On one very challenging day with Andrea, I received a phone message from my friend Sue. She said, "Do not worry; I have you covered the rest of the day." She felt called by God to pray His protection over me. She bound a spirit of fear from consuming me, bound an anxious spirit from taking over, and bound what she felt was "a rushing spirit"—a tormenting spirit assigned to make me feel rushed, harried, and overwhelmed.

Sue prayed God's peace over me and God's arms wrapped around my entire being, inside and out. She prayed for the Holy Spirit to gently lead me and help me minister to each one of my students individually while keeping my focus on God and off of my worries. She prayed the Spirit would close my ears to the voice of the enemy and that I would feel the calmness of the sun rising in the morning and the serenity of the sun setting at night. It was at times like these that I felt utterly carried by God.

On Friday morning, Andrea's school counselor called me to tell me Andrea was ready to talk. The next day, Andrea enthusiastically agreed to meet with one of my friends (as a mentor) later that same day. I was so thrilled—would we finally make progress? However, in what seemed like an instant, her countenance changed. She withdrew, pulled into herself, shifted her tone and her attitude, and refused to talk. She said she had no interest in discussing her feelings. I was discouraged . . . but I was also hopping mad at the enemy!

I turned in my Bible to Ephesians 6. Recognizing the spiritual battle we were facing, I bound Satan in the name and blood of Jesus and commanded all spiritual opposition away from her. Peace came over me. By the end of the day, she agreed to talk after all! This scripture flooded my mind:

(She who) dwells in the shelter of the Most High
will rest in the shadow of the Almighty.
I will say of the LORD, "He is my refuge and my fortress,
my God, in whom I trust." Surely he will save you
from the fowler's snare and from the deadly pestilence.
He will cover you with his feathers,
and under his wings you will find refuge;
his faithfulness will be your shield and rampart.
You will not fear the terror of night
nor the arrow that flies by day,
nor the pestilence that stalks in the darkness,
nor the plague that destroys at midday.
A thousand may fall at your side,
ten thousand at your right hand,
but it will not come near you.
You will only observe with your eyes
and see the punishment of the wicked.
If you say, "The LORD is my refuge,"
and you make the Most High your dwelling,

no harm will overtake you,
no disaster will come near your tent. For he will
command his angels concerning you
to guard you in all your ways;
they will lift you up in their hands,
so that you will not strike your foot against a stone.
You will tread on the lion and the cobra; you will
trample the great lion and the serpent.
"Because (she) loves me," says the LORD, "I will rescue (her);
I will protect (her), for (she) acknowledges my name.
(She) will call on me, and I will answer (her);
I will be with (her) in trouble,
I will deliver (her) and honor (her).
—Psalm 91:1-15

I treasured this word in my heart and prayed. Andrea and my friend met and talked for an extended time, but when she returned to the house, she still had her walls up around her heart. More prayer—I continued to cry out to God to soften her heart and mind. And . . . eventually . . . breakthrough!

It went like this: Later that evening, Andrea and I spoke. We cried and shared our hearts with one another. She told me she had been hurt to the point that she felt she couldn't trust anyone. I prayed silently, desperately, *Father, help her trust You by the power of Your Holy Spirit. Amen.*

We talked about finding her a counselor and she agreed that she wanted one. At 1:30 a.m., we finally got to bed and I was convinced she knew God was going to heal us and He had a divine purpose for our family. I realized that my struggles with her had brought me to my knees and closer to the Lord.

God spoke to my burdened heart:

My Precious One,
You are weary and fatigued. You must learn to relinquish all to Me. You must learn to stop worrying about your lack of sleep. Do you not see that like everything else in life, sleep too, is a gift from Me? You worry about how much time you sleep. My time is not measured in minutes and hours. I divinely bless your sleep and resting time and then multiply its blessings and benefits when you give up your anxious thoughts and rest totally in Me. Do not rob yourself of this blessing. Learn to be an obedient and compliant child, trusting Me for everything in every area of your life. Then and only then will your life be filled to complete joy in Me. You still have so much to learn. Your journey is long, hard, and demanding but the more you learn to depend on Me, the easier the journey will appear to you. Even you will amaze yourself at the strength you find and the joy you experience. Stop your struggling and rest quietly in Me in the deepest part of your soul, for I am there, ready to meet you.

The next day, my children were at friends' houses when I got home. Andrea was supposed to call me at 4:30 p.m., and I had not yet heard from her. I headed to church at about 6:00 p.m., after leaving her a note to call my cell the minute she got home. I arrived at home at 9:00, and she was still out. I thought to myself, *She is like a bird flown from the nest before her time. Protect her, Lord, and me!*

At 9:30 p.m., Andrea finally called me and asked if she could stay until 10:00 p.m. I said no, and she did not argue—a miracle! Or so I thought. She did not arrive home until 10:15 and did not even offer up an apology. I confronted her, and although I was full of anger and I shed tears, I was not overbearing.

Andrea was remorseful. For us, it was a divine moment. I was amazed as God put the exact right words in my mouth to speak. I was able to set up concrete rules and a game plan going forward, and Andrea agreed to them! This was serious progress for us.

Thank You, Lord, for this sweet time.

My Precious One,
Stand firm with the Belt of Truth, wearing the Breastplate of Righteousness. Your feet are shod in the Shoes of Peace, for you walk on holy ground. Your helmet of salvation can never be removed. No one ever loses their salvation. You can't even take it off to cool your head!

The breeze of the Holy Spirit will bring you refreshment. It will cool you and restore you and give you new life. Hope will return when you feel broken and burdened. Then the battle will continue.

Your Shield of Faith will grow at each step of faith that you take. Do not set it down for even a minute. You must never take it out of your hand. It is your most significant weapon, especially at your time of rest. This is when the enemy hits the hardest—when you are least expecting it. You must stand on guard ready, at all times. You can still do this and remain in Me—rested, joyful, pure, full of faith. This is the secret of living a full life in Me.

Yes, love is a key to it all. It is the driving force of everything. Without love, everything else is worth nothing (1 Corinthians 13). It negates everything else that you have been given. These weapons are to be used in order that love might reign AND the battle must be fought in love, with love, that love might rule in all of the hearts of man.

We must return to battle to go forward with My plan. Stand firm with the Sword of God's Word, for it is the ultimate truth. Nothing, absolutely nothing, takes precedence over My Word. The sword in this battle is My Word, the Sword of God's Word! It reveals all. It is life's instruction book, and yet so many never open it to even look at its pages.

Do you not see that as you seek to know Me, truly know Me, all else will fall into proper perspective? My children can be so narrow minded when fleshy desires reign over their life. All becomes distorted. All is seen in the WRONG light.

I am the light of the world. Whoever takes up his or her cross and follows Me will have eternal life. Then and only then, will My truth be revealed. The truth is My Word. Follow Me FIRST—then all else will be right with your soul!

Remembering

Seasons came and went, as did the memories that went along with them.

Easter, for example, has always been one of my favorite times of the year. We get to enjoy the jonquils and daffodils, the tulips, the dogwood, and the redbud trees. East Tennessee is so pretty in the spring. God's creation is a gift to us, here and everywhere. It is a testimony of the goodness of our God. He shows us how He is pursuing us through the things He has created for our enjoyment. I think of Isaiah 55:12, which says, "You will go out in joy and be led forth in peace; the mountains and hills will burst into song before you, and all the trees of the field will clap their hands." Have you ever gone on a walk and been consumed with the beauty of God's creation? Truly, the trees do clap their hands and the birds fill the air with songs of praise to their Maker.

Before I met David, I used to take all of this for granted. I didn't really notice. But when I met David Wiley, he opened up my eyes to see what was around me. He loved the outdoors and he constantly pointed out to me the beauty all around us. It was much later, after David had gone, that I truly saw God's hand in it—a gift to me. And it was much, much later that I learned to give God honor and glory and praise for it.

One spring, a couple years after David had gone, I found myself recalling how he and I had met, and how he'd changed the trajectory of my life. I was thirteen, living at home in Washington State with my mom and dad, two younger sisters, and my brother. It was late spring or early summertime.

Our neighbors were Ann and Hank, and Ann was David's older sister. As a graduation present, they had presented David with a bus ticket: a hundred dollars for a hundred days, anywhere in the United States via Greyhound. He picked Seattle, which was about as far away from Tennessee as he could get! Since his sister and brother-in-law lived in nearby Medina, it was the perfect set-up.

Because David worked nights as a waiter, he spent his days at Medina Beach, right down the road from our home. Being a new teenager, I spent my days there as well, along with my brother and sisters. David spent a lot of time playing with my youngest sister, Kay, who happened to be the same age as David's nephew, Bruce. But it wasn't long before David started talking to *me*.

At first, I really didn't give him the time of day. I just really didn't get it. The whole neighborhood was so taken with him they flocked to him like flies to fly paper. He certainly didn't need my attention, so I pretty much ignored him.

One morning, I awoke to my mom talking on the phone to David's sister, Ann. Ann told my mom that David had to leave unexpectedly and had returned to Tennessee. Before hanging up, she let my mom know that David had asked about dating me. Ann told my mom her shocked reply to her brother had been, "David, she's only thirteen! Are you crazy?" (I looked like I was eighteen, but I was barely a teenager!)

Before this, I'd had a conversation with my mom about dating, and had asked her how she knew Dad was the one for her. (She told me she believed that God had just one man picked out for her and she knew it was my dad the very first time she saw him. She just had to convince him of it!) So, when my Mom told me that seventeen-year old David wanted to date thirteen-year old me, a thought passed through my mind quickly: *I wonder if David is the man God has picked out for me?*

More springs and summers came and went and sometimes David came and went as well. I remember watching Neil Armstrong land on the moon while sitting next to David Wiley.

All through high school, I dated a guy who became a National Champion pole vaulter. I thought *for sure* I was going to marry him. The summer before I was to go to the University of Washington as a freshman, I was sitting next to the pole vaulter, watching TV at our home in Medina, when David Wiley showed up at my door. (Actually, he never knocked. He just walked in and yelled, "Hello!" in his very southern drawl.) He and his best friend were stopping by on their way from Tennessee to Wyoming to Seattle before ending their trip in San

Diego. He would be stationed there for four years with the Navy. He walked in and found me wrapped in the arms of the boy I was sure would be my future husband (or so I thought). We visited for a bit, and then I sent them on their way with a casual, "Keep in touch!"

The first day I spent in the Kappa House on the UW campus, I received a letter from David Wiley. How he knew I had pledged Kappa, no one knows to this day! I felt sad for him. I figured he must be miserably homesick for Tennessee—no friends and nothing to do. So, I wrote back, mostly out of pity. I continued to date the pole vaulter, who actually competed in some track meets in San Diego where David ran track for the Navy. Ironically, he and David actually met and became acquainted.

That December, in 1971, my pole vaulter decided it was time for us to break up after three years of dating. My heart was broken, and I mean really, really broken. I climbed out of his VW Bug, tears streaming down my face, went into the house, and climbed into bed. I was thankful for only one thing: that the next day began my Christmas vacation and I would be free from school for a month.

The next morning, I awoke with sunlight streaming in my window, and I heard a male voice from up the stairs, in my living room. My heart started to beat quickly and I thought maybe my pole vaulter had changed his mind! I quickly brushed my hair and moved cautiously towards his voice. My jaw dropped when I saw David, not the pole vaulter, sitting on my couch.

I asked him, incredulous, "What are you doing here?" He told me he had some time off for Christmas and it was just too far to go home to Tennessee, so he thought he would spend it with Ann and Hank. I was blown away! In a matter of hours, I had forgotten the pole vaulter completely and my heart kept pounding right out of my chest. I was furious with myself for being so fickle, but I just couldn't help it! I realized maybe David was truly the love of my life—though God had revealed him to me five years earlier (I just didn't know it at the time!).

8

My Sweet Love

David pursued me. He never gave up on me. When I was thirteen, I ignored him, and he got to know my family. Instead of giving up, he got to know my boyfriend. He listened to what I said and acted on it. When I told him to keep in touch, he wrote me letters.

After I fell in love with him, he pursued me more. He wrote to me every day. He called me on the phone. He sent me presents and cards. He came to visit as often as possible, driving twenty-two hours straight from San Diego, California to Medina, Washington in his racing-green British TR6! He pursued me diligently. It changed my heart and I began to pursue him back.

There are many more stories to tell about our courtship, but my memory fast forwards here to our wedding in June of 1975. Fourteen members of David's family came from Tennessee for our wedding on June 28th. I remember David asking me if we would have a small wedding. I pretty much grew up in the same house, in the same neighborhood, and in the same church for my twenty-two years. I said, "I have eighty family members alone who will attend the wedding!"

His quiet response was, "Oh." Nothing more was said. Three hundred and forty guests represented my family and friends on that lovely, early summer day.

Following the wedding, we decided to remain in the Seattle area until August, when I would have an interview with the Knox County schools in Tennessee. In June, David had been offered a job teaching eighth grade social studies and he agreed to take it if they would guarantee me an interview. Whoever got a job first determined where we would live after we married.

After two months of visiting in Seattle, we drove across the United States in that little green sports car, pulling a U-Haul with all of my possessions and our wedding gifts. I had never been away from home more than two weeks in my life. My parents had made me live on the University of Washington campus just fifteen minutes away from my childhood home, but that hardly qualified as "away." I would have preferred to live at home. In fact, I came home just about every weekend and often times on Tuesday nights to eat dinner. I was a homebody!

Now, after marrying David, I was to travel 2,800 miles southeast. We drove about five hours and stopped in Eastern Washington at a state park. I got out of the car barefooted and stepped on a bee. I cried for the next twenty-four hours and then I was okay.

Ten days later, we arrived at the Wiley family home on Raccoon Valley Road in Heiskell, Tennessee. A few days after that, we moved into our own apartment in Oak Ridge. David's family was wonderful. They treated me like their own. I could go on and on about the ways they loved and served me—such unconditional love.

I especially remember the day we had a new couch, chair, and coffee table delivered. David's sister Mary came to let them in while David and I were at work, teaching. When we arrived home, it was all set in place, complete with a beautiful silver bowl filled with daisies. It touched my heart beyond words.

My dad called that weekend to check on me. He asked me how I was doing. I told him about the furniture and also that Mary had done all of our laundry for us since we didn't have a washer or dryer. He responded by saying, "I should never have worried about you. Someone always takes care of you."

And Someone always has . . .

I want to ask you here, my reader, do you know who that Someone is? He is my first love, Jesus. He is your first love as well, whether you realize it or not. First John 4:19 tells us, "We love because He first loved us." He pursued us before we ever knew He existed.

Jeremiah 1:5 says, "Before I formed you in the womb I knew you." Really think about that! He thought of you first! He thought of you and *then* He created you. He made you for a purpose. Do you know what that main purpose is?

I love the excitement in Psalm 96:1-3: "Sing to the Lord a new song; sing to the Lord, all the earth. Sing to the Lord, praise His name; proclaim His salvation day after day. Declare His glory among the nations, His marvelous deeds among all peoples." As I look back over my life and memories, I realize I still have so much to praise Him for, so much to sing about.

Do you have a reason to sing to Him? Do you have a reason to praise His name? Have you paid attention to His advances? He is your very first pursuer! I thought my pole vaulter was my first pursuer, but I now know He was not. Jesus began to pursue me before I was even born.

Revelation 2:4 says, "You have forsaken the love you had at first." The verse speaks to a church, but it also applies to us as individuals. We too need to ask, "Have I?" If we are honest, it's likely we all have at some point in our life.

I was devastated and heartbroken when my first boyfriend broke up with me, but I was in a perfect place to pursue the One who was pursuing me even before I was born. Around that time, I began attending a weekly worship service and Bible study with kids on my university campus. One evening, I ended up at someone's house after the service, and the encounter changed the trajectory of my life.

I remember being in the living room. It was quite dark, and I felt very alone. Then, I heard a low voice from the far corner. I couldn't see who it was, but I did see a silhouette of a guy sitting on a table with his legs drawn into him. He said to me, "So, when did you become a Christian?"

Whoa . . . when did I become a Christian? I've always been a Christian! And I told him so. "I grew up believing in God, I said. "I went to church EVERY Sunday whether I liked it or not." We prayed before meals. We prayed before we went to bed!

My aunts, my mom, and my grandma—we used to say all they talked about was God and their kids.

Then, I heard him say to me, "No, you haven't always been a Christian. When did you get saved? I mean, you know, the actual date and the time?"

I was floored! After fumbling around with some words I just said, "It didn't happen that way for me."

That was the end of the conversation. I don't remember anything else, but for the next week that question never left my mind. No matter what I did, I couldn't let the encounter go.

A few days later, on a beautiful sunny afternoon, I decided to walk down to the "Ave." I was talking to God, telling Him, *I just really don't get it. I just really don't know what to do. What did he mean?* So, I said to Him, *I commit my life to You. I surrender everything to You. Just show me what You want me to do.*

That day, I changed from being the pursued to also being the pursuer. It truly changed the whole course of my life! I spent my college years pursuing my true First Love, getting to know Jesus and embarking on an intimate relationship with Him. I shared it all with David Wiley in the letters that I wrote to him.

There is nothing more special than when God intertwines our relationship with Him and with one another.

Over time, I learned that the Bible is God's love letter written to us. As I pursued Him by reading the Bible, I got hungrier and hungrier to know more about Him. John 3:16 came alive to me ("For God so loved the world that He gave His one and only son, that whoever believes in Him would not perish but have eternal life"), and Jesus Christ became a real person to me. I saw clearly how God gave up His only Son to die for me. My sin became evident and I repented and repented. I was washed, cleansed, forgiven, and made new! I became His bride, dressed in white and perfect in His sight.

(You have probably heard of the Church being the "Bride of Christ." But we too, individually are His bride!)

When David took his own life in 1994, God told me that He would show me what it really meant to be His bride. The Bible verse He gave me over and over again says, "Never will I leave you; never will I forsake you."

I would turn to Him in my moments of desperation. I would cry out and say, "Just give me a word, just speak to me, just let me know that You are really here." I would pray, open up my Bible, and this verse would jump off the page. It is found in at least four different books in the Bible: Deuteronomy 31:6, Joshua 1:5, 1 Kings 8:57 and Hebrews 13:5 . . . and God showed them all to me over time. "Be strong and courageous. Do not be afraid or terrified because of them, for the Lord your God goes with you; he will never leave you nor forsake you" (Deuteronomy 31:6).

A friend shared with me that prophecy is a kiss from God. Prophecy is God's Word. When that verse or any verse seemed to be highlighted to me specifically, I knew it was a kiss from my Bridegroom.

Growing in Intimacy

Most of us know God as Father. He reveals to us in Scripture how He provides for us and protects us. You may have prayed and asked God the Father to calm your fears during a storm or provide a job for you or a loved one. You may have asked Him to heal you or keep you safe as you travel. But to most, the idea of God as your husband is a new idea. It was to me, too.

We are all born with a hole in our heart—an empty space that was created by God to cause us to long for Him. It takes a lifetime to learn what that longing is and to seek after the right one to fill it. We all have a need for intimacy. We were created that way. God gave us the gift of marriage to show us the kind of relationship He desires to have with His Church—Christ, the Bridegroom and the Church, His Bride. But one step deeper is "you and Christ" alone.

Isaiah 54:5 says, "For the maker is your husband, the Lord Almighty is his name." He longs to love us and care for us, sustain and support us. He longs to give us the desires of our heart, but we must delight in Him first. As Psalm 37:4 says, "Delight yourself in the Lord and he will give you the desires of your heart."

Before my daughter was born, I longed for a brown-eyed, olive-skinned baby girl. If you know my Andrea, that is just who she is. Before Josh was born, I longed for a blue-eyed, blonde-haired little boy. Josh isn't so little anymore at nearly six feet, but he is quite the opposite of his older sister!

In my morning times spent with the Lord after David died, He showed me how He gave me those desires. He chose to fulfill the deepest desires of my heart so I would see how deeply He cared for me. How loving He is!

How did I delight in the Lord? I pursued Him. I spent time with Him. I read His "Love Letter" to me. I studied the Bible, trying to learn everything I could about Him. I took Isaiah 50:4b to heart, which says, "He awakens me morning by morning, wakens my ear to listen like one being taught." I learned to give time daily to sit at the feet of my Bridegroom, Jesus, to pray and surrender my day to His guidance and direction. Over time, I learned that if you want a real relationship with someone, you shouldn't do all of the talking. You need to listen, too. That's why God gave us just one mouth and two ears!

Without an earthly husband to talk to, I realized that every thought I had was a conversation with my heavenly bridegroom. He heard everything I said aloud and everything I thought inwardly. He was and is so attentive, so kind, and so compassionate. He wants me to succeed and He is more than patient. He encourages me as I try over and over again. Romans 8:1 says, "There is now no condemnation for those who are in Christ Jesus."

He truly is the perfect bridegroom.

I learned from Song of Solomon, chapter 2, that His banner over me is love. He envelops me in His love. He is proud and unashamed of me, even now. He sees past my weaknesses and sees me as He originally created me to be. He sees me as perfect in His sight. He encourages me to keep going and never give up.

James 1:2-5 says, "Consider it pure joy, my brothers (and sisters), whenever you face trials of many kinds, because you know that the testing of your faith develops perseverance. Perseverance must finish its work so that you may be mature and complete, not lacking anything. If any of you lacks wisdom he should ask God who gives generously to all without finding fault and it will be given to him."

In light of these scriptures, I have learned that God is in total control of my life. Even after utter tragedy, He can see the big picture and I can't. It is my job to pray and ask Him for more faith so I can trust that, ". . . in all things God works for the good of those who love Him who have been called according to His purpose." (Romans 8:28). That is my life verse. He, my Lord, has my best interest in whatever takes place in my life, no matter how horrific or devastating—even the loss of David by suicide.

Do not be anxious about anything but in
everything by prayer and petition,
with thanksgiving, present your requests to God.
And the peace of God, which transcends all understanding
will guard your hearts and your minds in Christ Jesus.
—Philippians 4:6-8

This is my other life verse: "Do not be anxious about anything but in *everything* by prayer and petition . . ." Emphasis on *everything*! Not just the blessings in my life, but also the pain and suffering and heartaches. It takes a huge leap of faith to embrace this, but it brings unbelievable freedom—and a sense of peace and security that only my heavenly bridegroom can offer me.

I have learned that when I am down and depressed, there is nothing better for lifting me up than singing to the Lord. I turn on worship music and sing at the top of my lungs. I worship and praise and I THANK the Lord for every miserable thing in my life. I sing, I cry, and my tears turn to laughter. I feel cleansed and rejuvenated. Psalm 18:16 says, "The Lord reached down from on high and took hold of me; he drew me out of deep waters. He rescued me from my powerful enemy, (depression, etc.) from my foes, who were too strong for me."

When David died, it nearly crushed me to death! The enemy was too strong for me. I was overwhelmed with negative feelings and thoughts and often felt too weak to carry on. My life and my family, and my heart, felt like they were being ripped apart. But God, in His sweet sovereignty, reached down and drew me out of the waters. I didn't drown in my sorrow.

I must admit that, at times, I did feel like I was drowning. I also questioned God's plan for my life as a young widow with two children to raise—I felt completely alone! But God became my bridegroom. We have been on a journey together that has helped me and many other people to know the beauty of our Creator, Father God, and Husband to all who choose to seek and pursue the One who has always pursued us.

48

Listening and Praying

Back in 1971 was when I learned to listen. And I mean really listen . . .

After surrendering my life to Jesus and being filled with the Holy Spirit, I couldn't stop talking about Him. It wasn't long before my mom and dad began to discover this personal, intimate relationship as well. My mom invited me to attend a Holy Spirit seminar put on by the Catholic church in our town. We chose to attend a workshop on "Listening Prayer." It was the beginning of a most amazing journey.

The priest explained that listening to God was just as important, if not more important, than talking to Him. He suggested that we read just one or two verses of our choice, then listen intently and write down what we heard God speak. I was blown away. I was used to reading at least a chapter, if not more! But the next morning I turned to the book of Matthew, skipped the genealogy, and read Matthew 1:18. God spoke to me about the seed of Jesus being planted in Mary like the seed of Jesus being planted in my heart. From that point on, I was hooked. I wish I still had that journal but I didn't learn to keep my journals until twenty-five years later, about two years after David died (thanks to my friend Sue).

It was at that time that God began to teach me the power in praying. He told me, "*Even the smallest aggravations need to be turned over to Me. You must learn to leave all of your burdens with Me.*"

He started showing me all the ways He would care for me and bless me if I would just turn my problems over to Him in prayer. Around this time, I started having trouble with my car. (And here I was a young, single woman—with little-to-no automotive expertise!) This was a huge concern to me. But after much prayer, I received a brake replacement for free. I truly believe it was God showing me that He was my Provider! Time after time, God showed up in situations like this, showing His hand in my life.

I was able to purchase clothes on sale because God led me to the perfect store on the perfect day. I crossed paths with people I had planned to invite to Sunday school but didn't have time to call. Miracle after miracle occurred.

My friend Sue and I would pray the evening before special events at school . . . or not. When we didn't, chaos would reign! (At home, too.) I would see the power in prayer both because of it, and because of the lack of it. Prayer = peace. No prayer = chaos. It was as simple as that.

Yet, I longed for more. Still, I was lonely. At the end of February, two and a half years after David died, I was feeling spiritually empty. I begged God to speak to me. I heard:

My Precious One,

You have entered a season of rest for a time. Relish in it. Do not be anxious over it or the purpose will be defeated. Enter your prayers in this journal. Spend much time in prayer. I will give you more and the prayers will reveal much to you.

Prayer is your most powerful weapon and yet many never come to know the real value of prayer because they do not take the time to put it to work. That is why I urge you in My Word to "pray without ceasing." I literally mean don't ever stop! Communication between you and Me should be a never-ceasing activity. Even the air you breathe, the tears you shed, and the sighs you utter can be in prayer to Me.

I am your constant companion. I never leave you. I never forsake you. On the other hand, at times you don't even acknowledge My existence. Many go on in life with no concern for Me. They do their own thing until tragedy strikes. Then and only then do they come running back to me. And often they are still self-seeking instead of seeking to please Me.

What is your attitude? God-centered or self-centered? One needs to reflect on the attitude daily. Only through the power of the Holy Spirit can that attitude be altered. I am the King of Kings, Lord of Lords, and you, My precious one, are a child of the King.

Receive your inheritance. Do not walk away from it. Enter My presence. Be filled with My joy and be used by the One who loves you unconditionally.

As I began to interact with Him through prayer more and more in this way, He began to give me prayers not only for myself and my own family and situations, but for others as well. Here is one He gave me to pray for my church and pastor:

Father God,

I just stand in awe of You, filled with a heart of thanksgiving. I ask You to clean me out today. I want no sin to come between us. Help me to identify my sin the moment it occurs so I can confess it to You immediately.

Thank You, Lord, for dying for me that I could be saved! Draw more people to Yourself, Father, like never before. Allow us to smell Your fragrance. Allow it to permeate our nostrils so that nothing, absolutely nothing, will distract us from seeing You.

Begin with our pastor, Lord, right this minute. Prepare him to minister to Your people. Hold him now in Your arms, Father. Allow him to feel Your healing touch. Let him feel the warmth of Your presence surround him; minister to his every need. Bathe him in the Balm of Gilead that he might be healed. Then allow him to offer that healing to his sheep.

There are so many hurting, so many dying. They need Your touch, Father. I pray Pastor will be anointed with Your healing touch. Fill him full of Your joy and Your praise. May You encourage him, Father, so that he might encourage us.

I eagerly anticipate our time of worship, Lord, for I know You will be there! Amen and Amen.

Trusting God

I was praying fervently for Andrea, but worry seemed to consume me. It was at this time that God gave me Psalm 139 to study. (Read it now and it will bless you.) Here is what I wrote in my journal after I read it:

139:24   *Worry is offensive to God*

139:11-12 *Darkness is like the light to God.*
           Dark times can bring about blessings.
           Don't shun difficult times.

139: 1-6   *God knows everything about me.*

139:7-11   *I cannot hide from God, <u>ever</u>.*

139:13-16 *God created me and knew me before I was born.*

139:17-18 *I am always with God!*

139:23-24 *I must not be anxious; He knows everything about me and*
           even knows the tragedies in my life before they happen. I
           must trust Him to care for me each and every moment, for
           He knows ahead of time all that is going to take place.

As I thought deeply on this, I heard:

My Precious One,
I do know all about you and you must trust in Me completely. Stay in an attitude of prayer and you will be less anxious. If you remain in My presence, your eyes will be opened to see My plan for your life. You will be at peace no matter what. Trust Me. You were fearfully and wonderfully made. I have a perfect plan for you. Trust Me to use life circumstances to draw you and others closer to Me, your heavenly Father.

Pray and trust, I knew that was what I needed to do. But life's circumstances continued to be so challenging. I struggled to keep from despair. Each morning I would get up before dawn to meet with God.

———

One thing that brought me great strength and taught me to trust God was prayer with Sue. Unbeknownst to me, she had started praying that God would open up an opportunity for the two of us to pray together regularly. Six weeks after she started asking the Lord about that, we prayed together on the phone for the first time.

Jesus said, "Again, I tell you that if two of you on earth
agree about anything they ask for, it will be done for them
by my Father in heaven. For where two or three come

together in my name, there am I with them.”
—Matthew 18:19-20

Not long after that, God spoke this to my heart, and I wrote it in my journal:

My Precious One,
Joy, joy, joy in Me! I know all of your needs and all of your desires. You have entered a new phase. You have taken a new direction and it will increase your spiritual power a hundredfold.

I have prepared you. Prayer is the greatest tool you can use to stop the enemy. You will learn beyond your wildest imagination the power there is in prayer. For together you are stronger than one. Together you will break down the barriers of the enemy that earlier you did not even know existed. I have been preparing you.

Sue wonders why it has taken so long. It has not been long, my child. You were not ready. You needed to hunger and thirst for My righteousness first. You needed to long for My companionship. You needed to develop a relationship with Me first. Now we are ready to go forward together to fight the battle at hand. Put on your armor. Do not fear. I have gone before you. Walk in My footsteps as a child walks in Daddy's footsteps in the snow. Take one step at a time. Don't even look ahead. Set your eyes upon Me and I will lead the way!

By now it had been more than two and a half years since David's death. God was so good to continue to care for me and my children! One morning I received a 6:00 a.m. call from a friend from church, who awoke burdened to pray for my family.

It was such an encouragement to me to know that she had prayed. More and more I saw the power of prayer working in my—and my family's—life.

———

In early February, Sue woke me up on an early Sunday morning. She thought I had tried to call her. Her phone had rung a single ring at five intervals. We claimed it as a divine wake-up call and spent time praying for our church service and my lesson on fear that I would teach at Sunday school that morning.

On my run that morning before I was to teach, I saw a picture of the earth—light and dark, day and night. I saw people (prayer warriors) praying twenty-four hours a day, around the world. I realized that when I was sleeping, someone on the other side of the earth was awake praying. I realized someone, somewhere, was praying all the time!

My Precious One,
You can live a victorious life every day. Fill your heart with a song and sing praises with your lips. Look into My glorious face. The warmth of My radiance will give you life—and life abundantly.

Go forth and do what I have called you to do. Do not be driven. Do each task today knowing that it is a divine appointment with Me. You have too much to do but all will be well. Learn to be guided by Me. Learn to rest in Me.

Come to Me in prayer before each assignment. I will give you all the tools that you need. Return to Me when each job is complete. I will build you, refresh you, and prepare you for the next task at hand.

I know you feel the burden lifted. I see the smile upon your face. Seek My truth and the truth will set you free—and you, my child, are free indeed.

I couldn't wait to write this down in my journal. When I finished, I felt an unbelievable power consume me. I no longer carried my heavy burden. I felt light and free. I wanted to stay and dwell in His presence forever but I had to get up and go.

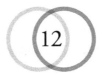

Learning to Fast

It was not uncommon for me to wake up in the middle of the night, around 3:00 or 4:00 a.m., pick up my pen, and write the things that were on my heart from the Lord. These early morning hours were when I heard Him speak most clearly to me. I was free from distractions and my mind was (mostly) at rest.

I had recently learned about the discipline of fasting, and was starting to practice it. One very early morning, while on one of my first fasts, I was awakened and sensed the Lord telling me,

My Child, My Precious One,
Your body is being prepared to do My work. I have called you to a time of prayer and fasting. Give no one else the credit. Record your stages of fasting and the lessons that you learn, for I will use you to teach others. The art of fasting is a lost art. My people must come to understand it again in these last days. Through your experience many will listen and then obey My call to fast and pray.

If you truly knew the full power of prayer and fasting, you would not be able to refrain from it or remain quiet about it. Fasting is a mystery that I am beginning to reveal to you so that you in turn may reveal it to others. It is a necessary tool in these last days to be used to fight against the onslaught of the enemy.

There will be much trial and tribulation these last days. My people must understand and use the tools I have provided for them. Fasting is one of these great and mighty tools.

The body is weak and submits to the flesh. It must be brought under control in order that My voice might be heard. It is in fasting that My voice becomes more audible and My plans are more clearly revealed.

Do not worry. I have a perfect plan for you. Trust in Me completely and show Me that trust by rejoicing at every turn.

Josh desires to visit a new church. Let him go. All will be well. A time will come when I will call you to go too. Do not worry about what other people think. Set your focus upon Me. You are to do My Kingdom work wherever I send you. You have not visited 100 churches yet. Do not tie yourself to any one person or any one place. I have freed you to move, wherever I need you.

I have chosen you because of your willingness. Cast out that spirit of fear. Stand up against it. I have given you the power to overcome. Allow nothing but My spirit to overcome you. I will lead you and guide you.

Do follow Me; I am your guide. I love you and care for you beyond any words I could use to describe. Know this and you will not be able to do anything other than what I have called you to do. Rest in Me. Seek My face and joy in your salvation, for I have saved you for a divine purpose, and that purpose is beginning to unfold at this very hour. ◯

I went back to bed and fell asleep, and woke up again at 6:00 a.m. to the alarm. I felt a bit shaky and weak, but not hungry. I felt God was answering my prayers and calling me to continue fasting. That day at around noon I wrote in my journal: *"It is prayer closet time. My body is not hungry but miserable. I keep wondering what good can come out of this. I feel like a space cadet—light headed, woozy, my heart pounding, weak eyes, bad breath. I chew gum and I never chew gum! Lord, I am being obedient. Teach me, Lord, I pray!"*

M y Precious One,
As you continue to fast, you will understand more and more. It is in your obedience to Me and the surrender of your will— mind, body, and soul—that you will hear My voice more clearly. We will become more and more as one, a unity of spirit. You will gain power that you have never before understood. You will find the two of us in one accord.

If My children would come to Me, submit themselves to Me by putting the flesh to rest, they would hear My voice audibly and obey it without hesitation. Just imagine the work that could be accomplished to further My Kingdom here on Earth if only My people would follow Me, truly follow Me. It is only in prayer and fasting that they will come to understand this revelation knowledge. I made it this way. It is in your sacrificial giving that you are enabled to receive the blessings that I have prepared for you.

So many miss the blessing because they never seek to find Me. Tell My people. Show My people. Some will listen and some will receive. Joy with them in their newly gained knowledge. Life is sweet. ◐

The next morning, I woke up rested and peaceful, except for my racing heart. *Why, Lord, does my heart speed up so quickly during a fast?* I wondered. *It just never seems to calm down.* It was my third day in a row of fasting—a new record for me. I prayed, *"Lord, I believe You will carry me through this day too, as I know that if you have called me to teach about fasting then I must experience it. Father God, thank You that You will not let me fail. Today I will be home more. Will it be harder? I need a miracle to sustain me and I believe You will provide."*

I believed the Lord would not allow me to fail. I believed He would carry me through, not allow my blood sugar to drop, to sustain me through the difficulty.

My Precious One,
You will learn more about your body than you have ever known before. Trust Me to teach you. Pay attention to what is going on and record it continually. I will teach you great and mighty things that you might teach others.

Your friend Sue will have some different experiences because every body is different. What she learns will be valuable to your teaching as well, so listen to her carefully and record what she has to say.

Yes, you are hungry today, but remain on your fast. The temptation will increase but only for a season. You must experience this to fully understand My chosen fast. Do not shun it yet. I am not finished preparing you to teach My people. Trust me completely. Be obedient and you will see the result—great stores of blessing will be yours to behold. I want to give them to you but you must first be willing to wait upon the Lord and renew your strength and then you will mount up with wings of angels. (WOW!! Do you mean angels or eagles?)

You will run and not be weary, you will walk and not faint. I am teaching you, Karen, to wait!

I was encouraged that Sue was fasting with me. It was easier knowing someone else was experiencing what I was, at the same time. It helped me to endure, even though I was not specifically aware of any pain and suffering on her part.

I was conscious of feeling self-centered, so concerned about me. I knew I had been consumed with my feelings, my "hurry-up-and-get-over-this" feeling. It was a rushing feeling; it made my heart race, and I hated it. I thought of David, whose heart raced like that for seven days before he died. His heart rate must have been even faster, because he couldn't sleep at all. I can hardly cope after three days of a racing heart, and my heart really didn't even race the first day. And mine was not a feeling of panic, like his was,

I wrote in my journal, *"Your voice, Father God, has become so clear to me. I don't want to stop writing. I don't want to get up. I don't want to leave Your Presence."* Then I reflected on the prayer time I had had with Him the previous night. My mouth had been filled with prayer. I could not pray enough . . . and then peace that flowed like a river. I wanted to bask in it forever. *"Lord, help me! I do not want to enter the real world. I feel weak and vulnerable. Please be my shield, my protector, and fill my vessel with You and only You!*

63

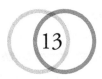

Prayer with Fasting

God began to teach me about fasting as a form of prayer. I was on a steep learning curve. One morning during this season, I wrote in my journal:

2:13 a.m.	*Woke up and prayed*
5:56 a.m.	*Woke up again and struggled to get up! I fell asleep on the couch last night. I am just too tired. Yesterday was a struggle. I fasted from wheat and sugar for a second day. It really reminded me to pray. It was pretty much a constant reminder all day. Denial is a funny thing. Cravings increase when you are denied.*

And then the next day:

4:59 a.m.   *Fasting from wheat and sugar is getting harder. I am eating more and I don't really need to. I often feel desperate so I eat something because of my emotional feelings rather than hunger. I don't feel like I focused on prayer as much today, but rather the out-of-control-like feelings. I was more negative, short, and impatient. Fasting is to shine light on your sin. Mine is shining through. Lord, cleanse me and heal me, I pray. This is my sacrifice to You.*

11:55 a.m.   *Fasting from lunch—prayers*

Precious Jesus,

Thank You for this time to spend with You in my little school closet. Thank You that my stomach is grumbling so my spirit might be fed. Thank You for my friend's obedience to fast for me today and the power I have seen in her prayers. My classroom is in total peace. It is pouring rain today and they are peaceful! I too am at peace.

The power in prayer and fasting overwhelms me, Father. Why is it such a well-kept secret? It is a deception of the enemy. Father, break the bondage of the people. Allow them to see the victory in prayer and fasting. Open up their eyes to see it and their ears to hear it.

The source of power in prayer and fasting that is available to us overwhelms me. Break through the murky waters, Lord, and let us see through the crystal clear, living waters, for You Father, are that water. Make me a clean and empty vessel that I might be cleansed from all fleshy desires and be filled with You—all of You! I want nothing less than to be filled completely with You—mind, body, and spirit.

I know it begins with me, Lord. I must be right with You first. Then I pray for all individuals at church. We need personal revival. Each heart cleansed and renewed—a right spirit, oh Lord, I pray. Then and only then can we experience corporate revival.

I am trusting, Lord, that it is coming. You are so precious to Me, Father. I glory in Your awesome presence and I thank You for using me. It humbles me, Lord, that You would see fit to use me.

Lord, there are so many lost and hurting souls. Bring them into my life. Open up my eyes to see and use me to minister. I give You my mouth, Lord; use it to speak only Your words. I give You my heart, Lord, to love only in the way You could love. Teach me to be discerning, and help me choose to do only Your work. I don't want to waste any of Your precious time. Use me, teach me, guide me, and direct me Lord. I am Yours!

On one of these early morning prayer times, I awoke at 3:57 a.m., hearing, *I am calling you.* Jeremiah 33:3 flooded my mind: "Call to me and I will answer you and I will tell you great and hidden things which you have not known." Everything in me did not want to listen. I did not want to write. I didn't want to get up! I did not have my journal but I had put paper beside my bed just in case, so I was without excuse.

Great, I thought. *Everything in my flesh rebels and then God speaks to me clearly. It is so embarrassing and so humbling. At first it doesn't flow. It keeps addressing me and my church. I don't get this!* I try to correct it. I just make a mess of it. I still write down pages and pages. *This message is for my church!! What am I to do with it, Lord?* The thought made me tremble. And then I fell back asleep.

At 6:00 a.m., the alarm awakened me, but I felt refreshed for the first time in a very long time. I quickly got ready for school. Later that day I shared my writings with Sue, who suggested I type it up and have it ready for Sunday—just in case.

Why does that thought make me tremble inside?

But I knew in my heart she was right. God had called me to fast and pray so the church would be prepared to hear Him and Him alone. Sue told me that she had received Romans chapter 11 when she was praying for me earlier. She was impressed with a vision of me teaching and writing a book. I was struck again by the enormity of that idea: God was teaching me right then and there to teach others!

> *I waited patiently for the Lord;*
> *he turned to me and heard my cry.*
> *He lifted me out of the slimy pit,*
> *out of the mud and mire;*
> *he set my feet on a rock (Christ)*
> *and gave me a firm place to stand.*
> *He put a new song in my mouth,*
> *a hymn of praise to our God.*
> *Many will see and fear and*
> *put their trust in the Lord.*
> *—Psalm 40:1-3*

He had lifted me! He lifted me out of that garbage dump. And He filled my whole being with a song. He taught me to rejoice in all things, even in the midst of the garbage.

Even though any of us may be in the midst of a struggle, even when we are really suffering, God can lift us up. We can see the mountaintop. We can look up and see the beauty even when we are at the foot of the mountain. We do not have to choose to live in the mud and the mire and the slimy pit. We can choose to stand on the rock while the slime rushes by us, like standing on a rock with the river water rushing past. If we slip and fall, we will die. The Rock keeps us above our circumstances even in the midst of our circumstances.

"Praise be to the King Almighty. Praise our mighty living God! My feet are planted on a firm foundation. Jesus is my rock and my fortress, the one in whom I live and move and have my being. He is my Lord and my Savior. In Him I surrender all. Use me, Lord Jesus, I pray."

God's Word to the Church

This is what the Lord, the God of Israel, says:
'Write in a book all the words I have spoken to you.
                                              —Jeremiah 30:2

As time went on, I felt God pulling me out of my own grief by pulling me close to His own heart, his heart for His Bride, the Church, and calling me to intercede. I sensed Him saying to me in my spirit:

My Precious One,
I am calling you—yes, you, to pray and fast for My people.
If My people, will fall to their knees and seek My face, I will hear
their cry and answer them. They have become a soft people, selfish

and desiring to seek their own ways. They must be willing to give up their fleshy desires and seek My will.

Set aside your own fleshly desires, pick up my cross, and follow Me. I cannot use people who stray. I cannot use a people that refuse to listen to My voice. My still and quiet voice is always heard in the quiet moments of resignation to My will, when self-seeking desires are set aside and your focus is on Me. Do not lose heart when it seems I do not speak. I never leave you. I will never forsake you.

Seek Me in prayer and fasting. Seek Me in My Word and by lifting praises of thanksgiving. "The LORD has done it this very day; let us rejoice today and be glad." (Psalm 118:24). Find joy in Me and joy in your salvation . . . for the day of the Lord is at hand.

Speak it to My people . . . proclaim it from the rooftops . . . All must hear of My saving grace. The time is short. Pray that My people will open their ears to hear. Pray that they will forsake their selfish desires and turn to Me instead. Pray that they will be given the strength by the power of My Holy Spirit to maintain the desire and the strength to fall down upon their knees and give Me praise and honor and glory even in the midst of their suffering. "'. . . if my people, who are called by my name, will humble themselves and pray and seek my face and turn from their wicked ways, then I will hear from heaven, and I will forgive their sin and will heal their land" (2 Chronicles 7:14).

I long for My Church, My precious Bride, to make herself holy and acceptable to Me. My people must humble themselves before Me. I want them to fall prostrate in My presence and seek My face. It is in prayer and fasting that they will come to hear My voice speak clearly to them.

This was a word I felt God giving me not just for me—but to speak to my church. Talk about intimidating! Though I felt overcome with fear, I went anyway. When I got to church, I was stunned to find out my pastor was speaking on overcoming fear that morning! I felt like God was talking directly to me. I knew I would some day have to share that message when God called on me. I remembered the words of the apostle Paul in 2 Corinthians 5:9: "So we make it our goal to please Him, whether we are at home in the body or away from it. . ."

In my mind's eye, I saw a vision of Jesus dressed in white at the back of the sanctuary. I was standing at the front of the church speaking to the congregation, but I didn't see them. My focus was on Him. I was the bride; He was the Bridegroom. I only had eyes for Him. (When your focus is on Christ, your fears leave you and your joy is made complete.)

I sensed Him calling me to fast again in preparation for sharing the word He had given me. I was not to share it that day, but was to wait for the time God would show me. With that in mind, I began studying the book of Daniel. When, in my quiet time, again I became overwhelmed with fear and anguish, and thought helplessness would surely overtake me. I read from Daniel chapter 10:2-19 (condensed below). It described just how I was feeling!

At that time I, Daniel, mourned for three weeks. I ate no choice food; no meat or wine touched my lips; and I used no lotions at all until the three weeks were over.

On the twenty-fourth day of the first month, as I was standing on the bank of the great river, the Tigris, I looked

*up and there before me was a man dressed in linen, with
a belt of fine gold from Uphaz around his waist. His body
was like topaz, his face like lightning, his eyes like flaming torches, his arms and legs like the gleam of burnished
bronze, and his voice like the sound of a multitude.*

*I, Daniel, was the only one who saw the vision; those
who were with me did not see it, but such terror overwhelmed them that they fled and hid themselves. So I was
left alone, gazing at this great vision; I had no strength left,
my face turned deathly pale and I was helpless.*

*Then I heard him speaking, and as I listened to him, I
fell into a deep sleep, my face to the ground. A hand touched
me and set me trembling on my hands and knees. He said,
"Daniel, you who are highly esteemed, consider carefully
the words I am about to speak to you, and stand up, for I
have now been sent to you." And when he said this to me,
I stood up trembling.*

*Then he continued, "Do not be afraid, Daniel. Since
the first day that you set your mind to gain understanding
and to humble yourself before your God, your words were
heard, and I have come in response to them. . .*

*. . . While he was saying this to me, I bowed with
my face toward the ground and was speechless. Then one
who looked like a man touched my lips, and I opened my
mouth and began to speak. I said to the one standing before
me, "I am overcome with anguish because of the vision, my
lord, and I feel very weak. How can I, your servant, talk*

with you, my lord? My strength is gone and I can hardly breathe."

Again the one who looked like a man touched me and gave me strength. "Do not be afraid, you who are highly esteemed," he said. "Peace! Be strong now; be strong."

When he spoke to me, I was strengthened and said, "Speak, my lord, since you have given me strength."

My heart leaped when I read this scripture how an angel (many scholars believe this was the pre-incarnate Jesus) touched Daniel and gave him strength. The angel—or perhaps Jesus, as it were—told him not to be afraid but to be at peace. I was encouraged that God would do the same for me. I wrote this prayer in my journal: "*Thank You, Lord, that I too will be strong when You call me to speak Your word. Thank you, Father, that I will be obedient, and that Your light will shine so brightly that no one will be able to see me. They will only be able to hear Your voice. Permeate their souls with Your Word. Pierce their hearts with conviction and allow brokenness to heal our land. Amen."*

The next morning, I was awakened abruptly and felt impressed that I was to write again, and that my pen and paper were always to be ready because I felt Him say to me, "*You always receive revelation following fasting."*

y Precious One,
Joy in Me. Joy in your salvation for I am your Father God, Heed my Word. Listen carefully to what I say for the time is

short and there is much to be done. The time is coming when you will rise and stand up before My people and speak. Many will listen and many will obey. You must set the example by being obedient to Me by rising and speaking the truth that I have put before you. Do not fear.

Remember, following Me is a choice. I long for them to choose. I long for them to hear My still, quiet voice, to develop a personal relationship of communication with Me, their Heavenly Father. They do not realize the blessings that are available to them. I long to bless My children. So many are hurting. The void inside of them is so great.

And yet some will still not choose Me. Their hearts have been hardened because of the sin in their life and because of the sin in the lives of those who came before them. Pray for forgiveness for the generations before you. Pray that the bondage of sins of the earlier generations will be broken and that generational curses will not be passed on. You have the power to ask and to receive. You are beginning to see the power of healing prayer. Yes, you can pray for healing and receive it. If you have the faith the size of a mustard seed you can move mountains.

Be bold. Be strong. Speak My Word and it will come to pass. There is power in My Word. You are a child of the King! Do not allow yourself to be downcast. Remain in a state of prayer at all times. Your faithfulness to pray will bring healing to the body for their are many sick and ailing parts. Just as you laid hands upon your own head and pleaded for physical healing, you must be willing to do the same for my ailing children.

Look for every opportunity to pray for others. Many will receive it and their faith will bring them strength and their bodies will be healed. Even those who do not receive it will be changed for the seeds will be planted and their hearts will be softened. Always be prayed up and prepared so that your spirit will be protected to give and to heal rather than to be broken.

Prayer is the most valuable weapon. Pray without ceasing! Through prayer, our hearts beat as one. Trust Me. Trust Me completely. The day is at hand!

A Time to Rest

It was now nearly three years since David's death. In many ways, we had all found our "new normal," but there was still much healing to be done. Things were still rocky with Andrea, as she continued to process her grief and anger internally and express it in ways that made our relationship difficult at times. Josh's response to the tension was to keep quiet and stay out of trouble. He felt responsible to not add to what Andrea was going through, and not contribute to my stress or the tension in the household. All three of us were trying to manage the pain in our own way.

It was clear we needed to get away, to be refreshed and reconnected, and for me particularly, to rest. I gloried in the opportunity to sit each morning on the waterfront deck in the hotel where we stayed in Kona, Hawaii, for two weeks, overlooking the ocean that pounded and rippled against the rocks.

One morning, I observed two little yellow birds that had just landed on the deck ledge. To my delight, they began to sing to me. In the distance, I could see two canoes, with eight people in each, paddling by in the distance. Fishing boats were everywhere. The horizon was bright and beautiful. The temperature was perfect. The sounds of the water hitting the volcanic rock along the shore while the birds sang was music to my ears. While I took all this in and reveled in the beauty and peace of it all, my children slept peacefully in their rooms behind me. It was heaven. I couldn't help but breathe deeply, trying to inhale the very Spirit of God, whom I felt so keenly in this place.

"Holy Spirit," I prayed softly, "come into me I pray and wash my sins away." I opened my Bible and turned to Psalm 97: "The Lord reigns, let the earth be glad; let the distant shores rejoice." And there I sat by the shores of Kona, Hawaii, just me and my Bridegroom. *Lord, you are so awesome, so glorious and so good. I praise you with my whole entire being. Praise the Lord!*

I sensed Him respond,

My Precious One,
The gloriousness that you feel is a gift from Me. Lean back against Me and rest your head upon Me. Breathe deeply and feel My Holy Spirit permeate your entire being. Deep within your earthly vessel My Spirit will fill you and revive you.

Why do you strive so hard and push yourself until you are depleted? You must learn from this experience, that healing comes when you allow yourself to draw apart and enter My presence. You do not need a vacation to be refreshed. You need to learn this method of healing in your day to day life. You need to set aside time for Me in the midst of your busy schedule. You must learn to stop and turn to Me instead of pushing on until everything is completed.

Over time, if you continue to strive, there will be no time for Me. The time is taken away daily, so slowly that you become deceived and do not recognize the cause of your restlessness and dissatisfaction. I am telling you now, draw apart before your day begins. Give your day to me and I will bless it. Draw apart at the end of your day to reflect back and give Me the glory and the praise.

But most important of all is to learn to draw apart in the midst of it. Give Me the situation, whatever it is, setting your eyes upon Me instead of the circumstances, and learn to praise Me for all things, in all places.

I slept so well while we were there—ten hours a night, which was remarkable for me. I fell asleep in the van on the way home from our day trip to the volcano. I couldn't believe how much all of us slept—Andrea, Josh, and myself. We obviously needed it; our exhaustion was physical as well as emotional and spiritual.

I wrote in my journal, *"This morning on the deck is totally magnificent. I think of the words of Scripture and they roll off my tongue in a song, 'Oh Lord, my Lord, how majestic is Your name in all the earth. Oh Lord, I praise your name, Oh Lord, I magnify your name, prince of peace, mighty God. Oh Lord, our God almighty.' They have flags set up for the regatta and we will have the perfect view from our balcony. The blue sky and wispy white clouds are breathtaking. The reflection on the water touches my soul. God, your creation is so mighty! Thank you, Father, for this most beautiful day!"* It was bliss.

Even in Hawaii, God continued to give me divine appointments to share the things He had been teaching me. One day, as I was out on our balcony, I noticed a girl on the rocky beach below sitting with her head down on her knees. I was so drawn to her that I began to pray for her. I heard God speak to me, whispering, *Go to her.* I continued to pray, and continued to hear in that still, quiet voice in my head, *Go to her.*

I opened my Bible to read but I could still hear God calling me to go to her. I argued with Him—*What will she think? What will I say? She'll think I'm crazy.* But, I wanted to be bold. And how could I be bold if I never gave myself the opportunity?

I also wanted to be obedient. So, I picked up my Bible and went, before I could change my mind, praying the whole way. I climbed over the lava rocks and headed out to the ocean's edge. I introduced myself and told her that God had told me to come to her. I shared my desire to be bold and obedient and asked if she was okay.

How surprised and delighted I was to find out that she was a believer! At that very moment, she had been praying for financial assistance to continue the YWAM (Youth with a Mission) ministry work there on the island. She was to be there three more months, but her funds had run out and she didn't know what she was going to do.

Delighted at God's goodness in connecting us, we prayed together, holding hands, heads bowed, at the ocean's edge, with ocean spray and waves breaking on the rocks. It was an incredible, awe-inspiring experience. I was drawn to this young woman like I'd known her all of my life, truly a work of God's Spirit. I promised to pray for her daily. I had a new and precious sister in Christ!

On our last day in Hawaii, I heard God say to me,

My Precious One,

Your rest here is about to come to an end, but your rest must continue. I long for you to learn to rest in My everlasting arms at all times and in all places. To be at peace in the midst of difficulty is a sign that you have learned to depend on Me completely. When you have obtained this, your joy will be made full.

It is for you to have. Reach out and grasp this truth. Hold on to it as if your life depended upon it. It is a life truth, a mystery that only those who truly seek Me can obtain. It is yours for the asking. I will teach you. This is the key: You can do all things in Christ who gives you strength (see Philippians 4:13), a verse you must live by.

You also must be assured in your heart that "all things work together for good for those who love the Lord and are called according to His purpose under heaven" (Romans 8:28). Remember, I planned your entire life before you were even created in your mother's womb. I knew it all before you were born.

You must accept this and live by it to experience the rest that I am talking about. Do you not see how you should be completely free from anxiety and at peace? If only you can grasp these truths. Joy will come in the morning and you will be at rest always.

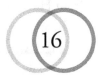

Praying for My Children

One day, during one of my wakeful times in the wee hours of the night, I received what I can only describe as a vision. In it, I heard a heart-wrenching cry. The pain was so deep and so agonizing that I wanted to bury it and never hear it again. I wanted to push it away. It was like a cry in the wilderness, like a hunted animal, and it was my own daughter! (It was at this point that I realized that I must open my eyes again and be obedient to journal my thoughts).

Andrea's pain in my vision was so deep and so intense that I could hardly bear it. She was calling out to her daddy and he was not there. She longed to be held in his arms. She longed to be comforted. And I could not console her. I could never fill that void.

My heart broke for her all over again and my tears flowed. I knew her pain was so intense, and it made my pain more intense. I knew her Father God was the only One who could heal that pain but she was running from Him. She wanted no one to fill that void but her earthly daddy, and he had deserted her.

I saw in my vision that anger was beginning to consume her. She ran in the opposite direction of where she should be headed. She was turning her back on God and He was weeping for her with compassion, His own pain intensifying. I could see He longed to scoop her up in His arms and comfort her, but sensed she first had to make the choice to turn around and look into His face.

I sensed God saying to me in this vision,

For now she will continue to run. As she runs, her pain will increase. The further she runs, the more intense the darkness becomes until the pitch black consumes her. Then and only then will she long to see the light once more. Then and only then, in her brokenness, will she turn to the light at the end of the tunnel and her life will take a turn for the better.

"She will begin to grasp that light a little at a time. She will begin to see more and more and she will receive the godly inheritance I have intended for her from the beginning of time. She then will become a light! Her testimony will make her whole. She too will speak to God's people with intense boldness. Many will hear His voice in the wilderness, will fall to their knees, and will worship God because of her faithfulness.

"Do not lose heart, my child: be strengthened through the power of My Holy Spirit. Be encouraged, for I have heard your prayers for your children and they will be answered. My people will be your

people and many will be saved out of your faithfulness and out of the faithfulness of your children." ◯

One day, not long after that, I reached into my basket of books and pulled out *Praying God's Will for My Daughter*. I prayed God would give me a scripture just for her.

I heard, *Turn to page 37*. I turned to it, and it was blank! At first, I was so disappointed and hopeless. Then I glanced at page 36—and was totally overwhelmed. Here was Philippians 4:6—"Be anxious for nothing," and 4:8—"Think on the good!"

My Precious One,
My child, your weariness comes from your own fretting and hopeless attitude. I have provided the means for you to overcome and I have continually spoken it in your ear. You must learn to praise Me and give Me thanks in all things. It is this complete trust in My will that will help you overcome. Apply these steps to your daily life:
1. *Do all through Christ*
2. *Pray*
3. *Give thanks*
4. *Rejoice*
5. *Be gentle*
6. *Think on the good* ◯

Journaling My Prayers

"Therefore, whoever humbles himself like this child
is the greatest in the kingdom of Heaven,
and, whoever welcomes a little child like this
in My name, welcomes Me."

—*Matthew 18:4-5*

Father God,

"A back-to-school promise, verses 4-5. Wow! Thank you Jesus. I can't wait to welcome my new class of students in a few weeks, in Jesus' name, so that I may welcome You too!

Lord, teach me and show me how I can be more of a witness for You. Protect me that I might share You openly and freely. Give me the words to speak. Allow them to flow through me. Do not allow me to hold back in the flesh, only in the spirit.

I long to be free, to freely serve You, to freely speak Your name. Teach me, Lord, to totally surrender my all to You, that nothing will hold me back from doing Your will and Your will alone. I pray in Jesus' name. Amen.

Journaling my thoughts, my feelings, and what I was hearing from God was incredibly healing. Sometimes He would wake me up in the night and I would journal through my prayer time with Him. Other times I would use my alone time in the first-grade classroom where I taught; I would retreat to my prayer closet.

My classroom was my mission field. I would pray all over it, sometimes in the Spirit, before the children arrived. I wrote about this in my journal to the Lord, *"My school closet is my sanctuary. I escape there at lunch to journal but sometimes I feel cheated from personal worship and prayer during the daytimes. You are teaching me again, Lord. Worship and prayer need to come first thing in the early morning before I ever leave for school. I will find a way. I will be obedient from now on. Thank you, Lord!"*

Recording my thoughts was so helpful, I was excited to share the practice with others. I began teaching a workshop at my church on prayer and journaling. One Saturday morning I wrote, "I am about to teach a session on journaling. It is a preparation for the church to hear the 'word' You gave me back in March. I will wait patiently for You, Lord, to call me to speak it." I sensed the time was soon when I would be released to share God's word with my church. I wanted to be ready.

I wrote, *"God, You are so totally awesome that I cannot even express myself. You are as the Bridegroom, for my entire being pants for You. I long to be in Your presence. I long to worship You with ever-increasing desire. I long to listen to Your voice while sitting at Your feet.*

I long for this relationship to grow in intimacy. The more You give to me, the more I long for. And, it is not tangible blessings I long for. It is You and only You, Lord. I want to walk with You and talk with You. I long for You to be my constant companion. I desire for You to never leave my side. I long to feel Your presence constantly and without shame.

Use me, Lord. Speak through me, Father, for it is ever growing within my soul. It consumes me, Lord, and there is no stopping it. Lord, You are in control and I long for You to remain in TOTAL control of my life! Teach me. Lead me, guide me, I pray. Then, and only then, will You be freed to use me to further Your Kingdom here on earth. I am a true, willing vessel.

Father, make me pure and white as snow. I long to be used by You in a powerful and mighty way. I am Yours. Father, use me from this day forth. I am eagerly anticipating. I will be watching to see what it is You have called me to do and I will be obedient because of the power of the Holy Spirit that is in me. Amen!"

Then Sunday, when I was to teach the ladies' class, it was a total struggle. My body ached all over. I had stayed in bed all day Saturday to rest in preparation; I needed to go to church and teach the class on prayer and journaling! Yet I didn't even have the strength to prepare my lesson. Again, I turned to my journal to cry out to the Lord, and wrote, *"You will have to provide the strength, energy, and time to do it today, Lord. I need another miracle, along with the voice to speak."*

That's when I heard, *Turn to James.* I turned to a section marked "patience in suffering." And I sensed God say to my spirit,

M y Precious One,

Rejoice, for I have awakened you to call you into my presence! You have moved up the secret stairs to a level few would even begin to understand. As you speak on journaling and your quiet time today, you must speak to the people at the point where you have come from. I will bring it to your remembrance. Be obedient to tell them My word, and challenge and inspire them to meet intimately with Me daily.

It will be by the power of the Holy Spirit that you will be able to speak. Draw ever so near to Me now that they might know that you have been with HIM. For it is by dwelling in My presence that You begin to reflect My presence. My light will shine upon you and the truth that I give you will reveal the darkness.

Joy, joy in Me. This is another divine appointment, another part of My plan that seeks to reveal truth to My children, and I have chosen you to speak and share this truth with others. Again, I say to you, give no one else the credit, for just as I use you, I also am using others.

You still have much to learn when it comes to viewing things through a spiritual perspective rather than a worldly point of view. Seek to grow. Allow Me to teach you. Knock, seek, and you will find many gems of truth . . ."

I responded in my journal, *"Father, I praise you and thank You for choosing me. It places me in total awe of Your magnificent grace. You are beyond my earthly comprehension. I praise You for sending the Holy Spirit to witness to me that I, in turn, may witness to others. Father God, use me and mold me; make me all You desire me to be."*

Then the next day: *"Yesterday my teaching the ladies' class on prayer and journaling was a blessing. Our prayer time for healing and anointing with oil was short but meaningful. I could write pages about it all but it was very draining. Lord, I must be doing something right. Thank you Father for Your protection. Guide me, I pray."*

An Opportunity to Give

My church—the new start-up congregation I'd joined shortly after David's death—was so, so life-giving to me. It was good to be part of something bigger than myself. It took me out of my own pain, and God used it to help me focus on His Kingdom instead of one of my own making.

I was excited to go to the leadership dessert we were going to be having, even though I was fasting from sugar. What a temptation! There we would fill out our pledge cards for the building fund.

I felt God telling me to give $22,000 in place of buying a new car, plus two hundred dollars above my tithe. This would amount to $29,200 over three years. But then, on the day of the dessert, I sensed Him telling me to give $22,000 immediately, that very night. I had heard this a few weeks earlier but had dismissed it. *Surely You don't mean now, Lord.*

I argued with God. *It will be embarrassing! No one else is giving money tonight! The first gift will be given at the service we're going to have at the mall.* But I had to be obedient. I deposited my check in the basket with my pledge card, though I feared it would be lost. *Chill, Karen,* I told myself.

It wasn't long before there was a tap on my shoulder. I turned to see the church treasurer standing in front of me, with tears in her eyes, saying my check had been an answer to prayer. It was the exact amount the church needed to get us into the mall on April 20th! The leadership team had been worrying about where the money was to come from. They knew they would get a great offering on April 20th, at the event, but didn't know what could be done before that.

Praise the Lord! God is so good! I really didn't know how to respond to that kind of miracle. This fasting and prayer stuff was new to me and I was just discovering the power it seemed to release. But I didn't want any credit; this was all God. So I kept it quiet and treasured it in my heart. I was just thankful to the Lord that I was obedient!

I wrote later in my journal, *"My cup runs over with joy! I am just bubbling over. I am filled with excitement. I literally cannot wait for this new church to become a reality. It consumes my soul because I was allowed to be a part of it. I want to tell the world. I want to shout it from the rooftops. This is the blessing of obedience. Oh Father God, use me more. Give me more money so I can give it away too. I feel so free—filled with hilarious laughter, for I know God loves a cheerful giver."*

"Remember this: Whoever sows sparingly will also reap sparingly, and whoever sows generously will also reap generously. Each of you should give what you have decided in your heart to give, not reluctantly or under compulsion, for God loves a cheerful giver"

—2 Corinthians 9:6-7.

Now he who supplies seed to the sower and bread for food will also supply and increase your store of seed and will enlarge the harvest of your righteousness! You will be made rich in every way so that you can be generous on every occasion and through us your generosity will result in Thanksgiving to God. This service that you perform is not only supplying the needs of Gods people but is also overflowing in many expressions of thanks to God. Because of the service by which you have proved yourselves, men will praise God for the obedience that accompanies your confession of the gospel of Christ and for your generosity of sharing with them and with everyone else. And in their prayers for you their hearts will go out to you, because of the surpassing grace God has given you. Thanks be to God for his indescribable gift!

—2 Corinthians 9:10-12

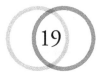

Praying in the Spirit

Praying in the Spirit, "in tongues," I found to be both a mystery and a love story. Basking in God's presence in that way was a feeling I'd rarely experienced before. It was an all-consuming love between me and my Bridegroom that was so powerful and so comforting all at the same time.

It reminded me of my fasting and worshiping experience years earlier, when I'd come home from a retreat and sent my family out to eat with friends, so I could fast, pray, and worship. I'd not had that kind of private worship experience again until I experienced worshiping in my prayer language.

I wrote, "*This time you are calling me to worship using my prayer language. I have never worshipped with 'tongues.' My prayer language has always been my tool to fight spiritual battles when I did not know how to pray. I would turn over my lack of wisdom to the Holy Spirit and pray in my prayer language, trusting, You, God, to provide me with the words to fight the battle raging in my soul.*

To worship in the Spirit? WOW! I just haven't had the freedom to do it!"

I began to look back and see. It was true; I hadn't had a lot of freedom in the area of using the gift of tongues. I remembered one of the retreats I'd attended with my mother when I was young, where a new Christian with the gift of tongues told me I was not truly baptized in the Spirit if I did not have the gift of tongues. It destroyed me.

I knew I had been prayed over, and I believed I had been given the gift of the Holy Spirit in spite of the lack of tongues. I remembered how I was in the room with a hundred others praying to receive that gift. I went home without the visible sign, but I knew I had been changed.

I felt God teaching me through these two experiences that not everyone's experience is the same. The new Christian who spoke so confidently to me at that retreat was too immature to know that her way was not the only way, and I needed to know this too! This truth has helped me to minister to others so many times since, and God has taught me not to be in bondage to man but to Him alone.

That being said, my first experience made me all the more determined to receive "the gift," so I returned home and soon found myself kneeling next to my bed praying earnestly to receive the gift of tongues and refusing to rise until I got it—and I did after much sweat and prayers! *God, you are so good.*

It began to change my prayer life from being shallow and meaningless to much more powerful. My whole life began to grow in spiritual wisdom and in freedom. And now, apparently, I was to worship in this new way as well!

I began to realize that there was a huge controversy over tongues. Some people accepted it and some were hostile against it. (I know now that the hostility came from the enemy.) I learned to keep my prayer language to myself and I used tongues only in private to pray when I didn't know how (such as when I didn't know the circumstances enough to pray or when I hurt so deeply and didn't know the cause). Praying in tongues would release me from my burden like nothing else.

So many times in my life I have been with wonderful Christian people who, through Bible study or discussion, would condemn the gift of tongues. My face would always turn crimson and I would pray that they would not discover my secret. I was embarrassed for my Lord and for those questioning God's Word—and for me, the one caught in the middle, ashamed of my embarrassment and my lack of boldness to stand up for the Word of God. I was afraid to share my well-kept secret and the power that tongues can bring to one's prayers, the healing it brings to one's body, both physical and spiritual, and the love and joy that overtake your entire being. It is a feeling that can only be experienced, but it offers you a complete sense of freedom!

Lord, help us to learn to know you better, and to be bold with ALL the gifts You have given us!

Sharing God's Word for the Church

It was a Sunday evening service, much like any other, and a Communion Sunday. After his sermon, our pastor brought the congregation into a time of confession and repentance to prepare us for the Lord's Supper. I could feel God's anointing on the church; we could all feel it. The praise and worship were amazing.

Then the pastor announced in a booming voice, "We will hear God speak tonight.!" The Holy Spirit and fear pulsated my body. *Tonight is the night!* I felt covered, sitting between friends, and so protected. My praise was *so* free. I prayed God would carry me forward at His appointed time. I prayed my pastor would be used to call me forward.

He did just that, as we finished praying. He asked if anyone felt led to confess their sin publicly, or to share. "SHARE" spoke to me and I knew this was God's calling to me, but that I had to wait until last—though I felt driven to go first.

I had spent time that night begging God to let me share the word He had given me. What a change from even the previous week! It had been more than a month that I had carried that burden to speak, and now I longed to get it over with and release the fear that gripped me.

Someone else shared and I heard very little. Then, no one else came. I worried about the congregation listening to the four pages I had to share; how could they remain attentive? My pastor had already spoken and I could feel their restlessness toward the end.

I waited almost too long; as I started up to the platform, the pastor cracked a joke that the call was over and I had missed out. But I didn't hear him. I simply smiled and said I needed to go up to the podium to read. I wasn't even sure I would be able to stand. I clutched the microphone hoping it would hold me up, and asked everyone to close their eyes so they wouldn't see me, and would instead listen to God. I began to speak.

I was aware that my voice, trembling and filled with fear and emotion, didn't even sound like me. A friend stepped up to the stage to support me and to hold me up, and I was so grateful for her presence. I did not even know who it was until I was half-way through. Then, I began to weep, but the tears were not mine. They were God's tears.

I felt almost removed, looking on rather than participating, yet I felt my energy drain, though my voice increased in intensity. When I finished, I could not move. I closed my eyes and prayed and prayed. I turned to my friend standing next to me after silence had gone on for what seemed like an eternity.

Would my pastor take over now? I wondered if he was allowing people to pray and repent or if he just didn't know what to do with me. I imagined it was both. He did finally get up and start speaking, but I didn't hear him. I was depleted.

My sweet friend hugged me and whispered in my ear to always listen to God and to always do whatever it was that He was calling me to do. WOW! I left my "word" and walked back to the pew with eyes cast down. I desperately longed for no one to see me, although I knew that was impossible.

I heard sniffling sounds around the sanctuary. Everyone was broken! If there was a dry eye, have mercy on the soul that did not receive that word from The Almighty. I buried my head in my hands, and felt friends surrounding me and touching me, which brought me comfort. I felt distant, disoriented, unemotional— even though I'd just experienced every emotion.

It was not that I was not really experiencing them; I was just the vessel in which everything had just passed through. It is not possible to describe it. I wanted to cut a hole in the floor and drop into it and flee. I dreaded having to face anyone, so I remained in a state of prayer and confession and prayed for the brokenness of the people in our church, myself included.

The bread was passed for communion and Sue knocked into it and spilled the bread on the floor. God spoke to her and told her it was the overflow from our obedience, just as her prayers for me right before had overflowed with His love and compassion. Praying in the Spirit at church. If they only knew! The spill made me laugh and I so needed to laugh! Communion time was a blessing that night.

I told God, *"Lord, Your timing is so perfect. We needed to hear this word before moving to our new location at the mall. I pray Your children are being obedient to You this week, fasting and praying and seeking Your forgiveness. We need to enter our new building with pure, clean, white, and holy vessels. Change us, oh Lord, I pray!"*

At the end of the service, the pastor announced that someone had left the sanctuary, at the beginning, to seek salvation. God was moving. That person returned at the end and the pastor's wife introduced the new Christian who had just asked Jesus into his heart! She announced that his school teacher (me), had invited him to church.

Again I whispered to the Lord, "I am blown over, God, You are so mighty. You took them out of there for almost the whole service. They were not there when I spoke Your word. You are my protector and my shield. Then you blessed me with a lost soul who has entered Your Kingdom! I pray that his heart will be changed completely and that he will surrender his entire life to You. This family needs healing, Lord, and You have placed them in my life for a reason. Protect me, Father. Lead me and teach me through these relationships."

People began asking me to pray with and for them. I was so grateful to the Lord for giving me a mission. I could not bear to stay and be the center of attention. A teen stopped to tell me about the whipping Christ received and how her Sunday school teacher spoke about the crown of thorns, and what that meant to her. *Father, you have touched her deeply.*

Sue and I prayed together for our friend, whose son chose not to take communion and she was devastated. I immediately rejoiced (through spiritual eyes), because I knew he realized the seriousness of taking communion when unforgiveness was harbored. Sue and I encouraged her—God was at work!

When we returned to the sanctuary, I saw to my surprise that it was still full. People didn't want to leave the glory! A couple stepped up to thank and encourage me, people I didn't even know. The man said the best part was closing their eyes. He said if I hadn't asked them to do that, they would have seen me instead of God. WOW! This was more confirmation and such an encouragement.

The next day, I received this during my morning prayer time:

My Precious One,
Joy in Me. Joy in your salvation. You are weary from your divine appointment of yesterday. You were my obedient child to do as I called you to do—to rise up and stand before my people and speak my word with boldness and truth. The word touched many, many hearts and lives will be changed. The church will become the church I have called it to become.

People's hearts have been softened and healing will come quickly to their land when they heed My call and follow My ways. I have called them to fast and pray. Teach them, my child. The opportunity will come again. Remain in a state of readiness and accept the call to teach immediately without hesitation. I will work out the other responsibilities that you have taken on.

This will not be easy and you will be tested. Keep to the straight and narrow path. I will lead you. Set your eyes upon Me. Do not take them off. Remain in My presence at all times and in all places.

I long to care for you! I long for our communion to be so intimate that we march into battle as one. It is your choice. I am offering it to you, but you must remain with Me forever, like a divine union of marriage, a covenant not to be broken.

You must be completely released from the bondage of man. Do not fear what others may be thinking. Always seek Me first before you respond to anyone. Check your emotions and do not follow them. Set your eyes upon Me and speak to Me, for everything else follows prayer. ***Prayer must come first****. Be obedient to this command and boldly call My people to follow. Go out and obey My Word, proclaiming it to my people now and always!*

Starting to Speak

After that, I was invited to speak at our church's upcoming ladies' retreat. I was so excited! I felt God say to me,

My Precious One,
Rest completely in Me this new day. It is a time of rest and renewal for your mind, body, and soul. Joy in My presence. Look to me for guidance and direction. I will lead you and show you what I would have you do this day. Every day is a gift from Me. Treat it as such.

Do not waste the time that I have given you. You have much to accomplish—mundane tasks must be addressed, but do all to My glory. Worship and adore Me in all that you do. Set your focus on Me and all will be done more swiftly and to completion with very little challenge or frustration. Believe this and act upon it and you will see how I work and bless you even in the smallest of tasks.

You are My child and I love you with a deeper love, one that your mind cannot possibly fathom. Put on your praise music. Put a song in your heart!

I responded in my journal, "*Father God, I long to worship and adore You. I long to lift up my voice in praise to You. You are my Lord and my King. You are precious in my sight. Allow me to feel Your presence that my joy might be made full.*

Lord, Father God, I have so much that I would like to accomplish today. I am so grateful for finishing my banking yesterday. You're right; I am accomplishing a lot! God, You are so good. Show me today what You would have me do. I really feel the need to plan my fifty-minute retreat talk. Father God, reveal to me just exactly what it is that You want me to share."

What I really wanted was a nap! I let the retreat committee know that God had called me to teach on fasting. They were very encouraging. I was so glad I had gotten out of bed at about 12:30 a.m. to get my journal in preparation to write. I knew the Lord would wake me in the morning because it was my fasting day for my church and I eagerly anticipated it.

The next day I started early as expected and spent most of the day preparing my fasting presentation for the ladies retreat. It totally excited me. The words just flowed onto sixteen pages and I was only half-way done. When I finished it, I timed it and it was perfect for my allotted fifty minutes.

My journal was such a source of information; the sheer amount of content in it, was almost overwhelming. All that I had learned in the short time since David's death, and since I started listening and praying, would have all been forgotten if I had not journaled. I was so grateful.

I thought, *This is a book of my life with you, Lord, and there is so much more in it to share.* WOW! My prayer to have a testimony came to mind. This fasting presentation was my testimony, and I knew it would be so much more entertaining than just plain factual information like that given in most presentations. I thought again how a friend once told me, "You are going to teach it." *Thank you, Lord, for calling me to experience fasting so that I could teach it.*

I did love to teach! I looked at my life since David's death and saw my answered prayer to have a testimony. My life, every day since, had become a testimony. I now see that my life before his death was a testimony too, but as time has gone on, the testimony of God's faithfulness has become far more powerful. *God, you are so powerful. God, you are so good.*

As I continued to study, I could see more clearly the power in fasting. I was convinced that everyone needed to hear this. I was simply sharing my life with them. I felt almost ashamed because the preparation was so easy and brought me so much pleasure. *God, you totally amaze me.*

The time factor did overwhelm me. It was taking so long to write it all down but, again, I thought of the pastor, who spoke at a retreat I once attended. He told me he always wrote down every word in his sermon ahead of time. This was confirmation to me that it was okay for me to do that too. God always did that for me before my Bible study lesson, and now I felt encouraged to do the same with my retreat talk.

It was ironic, because I used to really frown on pastors who came to the pulpit with everything written down. I wondered how that could leave any room for the Holy Spirit to move. Now I knew firsthand how He could move in my heart during preparation AND during the presentation. *WOW! God, you are awesome.*

I reached out to contact as many women as I could, to encourage them to attend the retreat. As I did, I found each one unloaded on me their present struggle. Everyone, it seemed, was struggling! I prayed and prayed and continued to fast as I prepared.

*There is **so** much that I want to do, Lord; guide me, I pray.*

When the retreat finally arrived, it was a total struggle trying to get there. Sue and I arrived forty minutes late! But once there, we got straight to prayer and it was as if the heavens opened up and God descended upon us. Our worship time was so special. His presence was awesome—*is* awesome. The first speaker's topic was on spiritual warfare. It was going to tie in perfectly with my talk on fasting.

After the first sessions, I sat on the balcony of my room, overlooking the river and viewing the mountaintops. It was breathtaking! I thought of David and his desire to always be in the mountains, close to the Father. We all desire to stay on the mountaintop, but it is in the valley where we really learn to meet Him.

I prayed aloud, "God, I pray for these ladies that You have sent here. They are here for a reason. I keep thinking of the verse in Isaiah 55 that says fasting will bring healing quickly. I really feel led to bring that out today and it is not in my lesson plan.

"Father God, speak through me, use, me, guide me, direct me. Show me when You want me to share that verse and do not allow me to fail to be obedient. I give You my mouth. Use me, Lord. Speak through me—your words, not mine. Father, let these ladies see You, Lord, not me. Let them feel no condemnation but rather encouragement to try. Reveal this mystery of fasting to them, Father, that the bondage of any sin will come to the surface and be revealed.

"Lord, I feel so weak and so inadequate. And, fear is coming upon me. Lord. Deliver me from this fear and this weak state of mind. Fill me with Your boldness, boldness to speak and proclaim Your Word.

"God, you are so awesome. I long to become all that You want me to be. Show me, guide me, teach me, I pray. I am Yours, now and forevermore. Amen."

The next morning, we gathered again to pray together, all the speakers and Sue. Someone prayed for my stomach problems, for healing. *How did they know?* I felt God's strong presence. But when we finished and everyone left, I pulled Sue back into the "prayer room." I told her she had to pray for me more, because I was a wreck!

Sue prayed for peace, and for deliverance from "whatever" needed to be loosed from me. I immediately felt the fear leave!! She mentioned fear and condemnation—just exactly what I needed deliverance from and didn't know it myself. God had given her discernment—praise the Lord! I was freed, and my stomach gave me no more problems the rest of the weekend. I was ready to praise, and to speak.

Our group of forty-five was divided into three groups of fifteen, and I was to speak fifty minutes each time. Sue went along with me each time to pray while I spoke. Throughout that day, I ministered to many women, and God performed miracles!

At one point, a woman approached me and asked me if I had ever considered writing a book. This blew me away. It wasn't the first time it had been suggested to me. *Why, oh why, Lord am I so slow to accept Your guidance? I just feel so inadequate. I feel so incapable. I can't imagine doing such a huge task. I wouldn't even know where to begin.* The woman felt impressed to tell me I needed to write my fasting talk down; I told her I already had.

"I've never felt the presence of God quite like I did when you read that word God gave you for us," she said. "It was like you weren't even there, but instead God was speaking to us through you." *Wow! Answered prayer! Lord, you are so good to me. It overwhelms me that you would choose to use me!!*

The retreat was amazing—and sharing what my Bridegroom had taught me about fasting was even more amazing. Sunday morning, Sue came to pick me up and we prayed and praised all the way to church. *Can we stay on this mountaintop forever?*

At church, we sang of the Bride and Bridegroom. We, the Church, are the Bride. Jesus is our Bridegroom. *"Jesus, You are my Bridegroom and my love for You can no longer be contained. My cup overflows. I am filled to overflowing with Your presence. I am aware of no one. I have entered Your Holy of Holies. I don't ever want to leave. My fasting was a sacrificial offering to You, and now You have called me to Your banquet table for a feast. I don't want physical food. I want spiritual food. Blessing always follows fasting. To God be the glory!"*

The entire church service felt anointed, and the sermon spoke directly to my heart. It was a message on the importance of how we spend our time here on earth. How timely! I prayed silently, *"Father God, there are so many physically hurting people at church. We need a healing ministry. There is much work to be done and Your children are wounded, and wounded soldiers only add extra burden to the battle.*

"Lord, don't let me stop interceding for these people. I need more discernment. I need to know how to pray spiritual warfare prayers. The battle is raging and I need this tool to fight. I even see the need in my own family. My children often gang up on me. It is so not them, but they are being used by the enemy at times to undermine me. I often feel knocked down. Hear my prayers, Lord! I know we will be a team again one day, bold, strong and witnessing for You, Lord."

God Is in Control

My Precious One,

I hear your prayers for your children and your prayers will be answered. Speak them in faith, knowing and believing that all You ask in My name will come to pass when you choose to pray My Word, the Scriptures. There is unbelievable power in My Word.

If only people understood the power of the unity of prayer and My Word, it would be the only words that would flow from their lips. Mountains would be moved and walls would come tumbling down. There is tremendous power in My Word. Seek My Word in time of distress. Locate My promises to you and claim them in the midst of your pain. Call them out in your trial and they will provide hope.

My Word is truth and truth will break down any barriers of mistrust. My Word will bring healing to hurting souls. It is like the Balm of Gilead. It washes away the hurt and pain and provides a healing, soothing oil to the soul. It brings comfort. It is compassionate, but it is also like a two-edged sword that will expose the darkness and cut the sin from your life. It always reveals truth. When, and only when, truth is revealed, healing can begin. Seek My Word, read it, study it, absorb it, memorize it. My Word is Me."

Oh, how I needed that word, that assurance, from my heavenly Father. I prayed regularly with and for my children, but still they struggled. I wrote in my journal, *"I just prayed with Andrea for protection and guidance today. She seems fearful and lacks joy."*

I heard:

My Precious One,
Your faith is increasing right before your very eyes! Do you see how I use every situation in your life to teach you and refine you? Shun nothing that comes to you, but instead, watch eagerly to see how I will use the seemingly impossible or discouraging situation to bring glory to My name.

Your focus on Me will release My power to curtail the situation more quickly and effectively. I am in control! Walk it, speak it, believe it, hold onto it. I know all things before they take place and I know the outcome before anything ever begins. I am your Father God, and I love you with a deep and everlasting love. Trust Me totally and completely. It is a choice you must make daily.

Pick up your cross and follow Me. Be careful not to stray from the path. Do not turn to the right or the left, walk on the straight and narrow. You can do this successfully only if you refrain from taking your eyes off of Me. Set your eyes on Me and remain in My presence forever. Amen." ◌

I had my faith tested many times over. I remember praying and sending my Andrea on her way, so many times not knowing if she would come back through my door. I remember one day in particular I received God's unbelievable peace in the face of my fear as I prayed, but when she hadn't returned at 1:00 p.m. from her 10:00 a.m. appointment, I became concerned. At 2:00 p.m., I fought panic inside. She didn't arrive until 4:00 p.m., and I heard . . .

M y Precious One,
My child, you must believe with a childlike faith and not give in to fear. Most of my children give into fear and submit to the ways of the flesh instead of putting their faith in Me. You can do nothing on your own. But you can do all things in My strength.

If my children could just realize the source of their power and depend on Me instead of their own self sufficiency, great things would be accomplished for My Kingdom in a very short time. Seek now to learn these truths. Long for these mysteries to be revealed to you and seek My face and My power will be revealed to you. Much must be overcome before you will have the full use of My power.

Through this season of suffering, you are being refined, molded, and made into the person I long for you to be. If you will seek Me and My ways and be obedient, the lessons will come more quickly and the refining will be accomplished more rapidly.

How willing are you to receive what I have for you? How willing are you to suffer for My name's sake? Reach out and take My hand. I will go with you. I will encourage you. Just don't take your eyes from My face. If you remain in My presence, the pain will always be bearable. It is when you choose to leave Me that you seem to be crushed. It is this reliance upon Me that keeps your head above water. Set your eyes upon the light. It will lead you out of the darkness and into My presence, once again.

Looking Back and Looking Ahead

I sat on my porch, my sanctuary, for the first time that summer, in August of 1997. It was now a full three years since David's death. It was so peaceful, so beautiful, to be surrounded by God's creation, with its promise of resurrection and new life.

Amidst all of the beauty I was fixated on one ugly dead tree. It was right in front of my face. I wanted to cut it down and get rid of it right then and there—it was spoiling my view! But I felt such a sadness because it used to be a beautiful dogwood. I wondered, *What killed it?* I marveled that this one dead tree could keep me from noticing the beauty around it.

I was struck by how other "dead trees" in my life often did the same thing to me. I knew I needed to learn to focus on God's whole plan instead of the immediate trial I was in at the time, or all I would see would be the dead wood. I prayed, *"Lord, allow me to always look past my circumstances and see things the way You see them. Open up my spiritual eyes, I pray in Jesus' name. Amen."*

I heard:

My Precious One,

Trust and obey, it is God's only way. Set your eyes upon Me and you will have peace. Look at the dead trees in your life through spiritual eyes, see them as I see them. I can heal, renew, and revive. The dead tree is really a beautiful dogwood in full bloom.

I will restore My children. I will restore your children. I will put new life into them. They will bud and bloom, and flourish once again. You must trust Me. You must obey Me. You must allow My plan to unfold without allowing your fears to overtake you and lead you into taking over My work. Otherwise, you will get in My way and the plan will unfold more slowly, and you will be allowed more time to be frustrated. Leave it all in My hands. Trust Me completely. Joy in Me. Joy in your salvation and the salvation of your loved ones."

Is any one among you in trouble? Let them pray. Is anyone unhappy?
Let them sing songs of praise.
—James 5:13

You are never alone, for I am always with you. When you feel alone or afraid, turn to Me. Set your eyes upon Me, rather than upon the problem. Clear your mind of anxious thoughts and fill your mouth with praise. The joy of the Lord will be your strength. The joy of the Lord will overtake you. Your entire being will be filled up with the presence of My Holy Spirit and your joy will be made full.

You can enter My presence at any time and in any place. There are no spiritual limitations. The limitations arise from within. your own SELF. Self is that which blocks communion with Me, your Heavenly Father. Be filled with praise, and joy will come in the morning. It will come forth, overflow, and pour out to those around you, even in the midst of difficult circumstances.

Remember this: times are not so tough now but this truth will bring life to your soul in the midst of the difficulties you will face in the future.

Your time has come and more and more your ministry is being revealed to you. Your eyes are being opened to see spiritually and My plan for you is becoming clearer.

Continue to pray for more faith, wisdom, and discernment. It will allow your spirit to soar and receive all I have to offer you. This journey you are about to take is one that will lift you to new heights. Bind that spirit of fear that tries to sneak in when you have new adventures in your life. I will never leave you or forsake you. I have gone before you to prepare the way.

All is in My hands. It is your job to trust Me and obey with childlike faith. Hold on to My hand and look into My face. Step into My footsteps and you will have no fear, for you know that I would never lead you astray. There is much work to be done and I need My willing servants to follow Me into the promised land.

You know that there will be a wilderness first and that there will be a struggle to reach our destiny. But, all will work together for good for those who love Me and are called according to My purpose under Heaven. Rejoice, for you, My child, are a part of My divine purpose and you are walking in My footsteps. You are a part of My perfect plan.

Continue to pray for more workers. I will place many in your path who are eager but need to be trained. Be ready to speak My word at the drop of a hat. My words are your words if you deem it so. Rest assured; I will use you if only you choose to be ready and willing. Rejoice in your new-found journey. It is ready to unfold. Be alert. Be receptive, for it is unfolding NOW!"

This was such an encouraging word. Though at times I had felt alone, I knew I never really was. And I could already see the results of pruning in my life, although I realized there was probably more to come.

I was strengthened in knowing that My Heavenly Father, my ultimate Bridegroom, was with me. He was providing for me, and for Josh and Andrea. His love surrounded us in so many ways.

I couldn't control my circumstances, but I could control my responses to those circumstances. I could choose to stay close to the One who held everything in *His* control.

And that was enough for me.

Epilogue

Jesus said to her, "I am the resurrection and the life.
He who believes in me will live, even though he dies;
and whoever lives and believes in me will never die."
Do you believe this?
—John 11:25-26

Jesus wept. . . . Then Jesus said,
"Did I not tell you that if you believed,
you would see the glory of God?" When he had said this,
Jesus called in a loud voice, "Lazarus, come out!"
The dead man came out . . .
—John 11:35, 40-44

Before I came to know Christ, I had no idea of the true power of the resurrection life we have in Jesus. In the years following David's death, I came to know that power and came to know Christ even more intimately.

The "dead one" in the scripture above was me. Looking back now, I can see how God has strategically used these last twenty-six years in multiple ways: to comfort me, to teach me that He is my Heavenly Father AND my Heavenly Bridegroom, and to teach me how to live as His bride.

He also gave me the word to deliver to the Church, with the same message, that He is our Heavenly Father and our Heavenly Bridegroom. And He desires for us, the Church, to live as His bride.

We are predestined to be resurrected and live eternally with Him, for sure. But we are also filled with His resurrection life to live in intimacy with Him here and now. We are His bride on Earth, the Church—not just in the corporate sense, but each of us individually can know Him personally in this way.

I know your experience will not be the same as mine. He speaks to us all so differently and I encourage you to seek out the personal ways He will speak to you, too, if you seek Him. I only hope the thoughts and experiences I have shared here will inspire you in your own journey to know Your Bridegroom and experience all that He has for you.

—*Karen Lunde Wiley*
Knoxville, Tennessee, 2020

APPENDIX

Precious Thoughts

The following are some of the "Precious Ones" entries from my 1997 journals, following David's death, when God was beginning to teach me to live as His bride, and to know Him as my Heavenly Father and Bridegroom.

I've arranged them by topic and include them here for your encouragement, my reader, praying you, too, come to know Him as both.

—Karen

Prayer and Praise

"Do not be anxious about anything, but in every situation, by prayer and petition, with thanksgiving, present your requests to God. And the peace of God, which transcends all understanding, will guard your hearts and your minds in Christ Jesus" (Philippians 4:6-7)

My Precious One,
Do you see the formula here for peaceful living? It is so simple and so clear and can be applied at any time! However, my children continue to be anxious.

Prayer and praise are two powers that release My power. The world seeks peace in all the wrong places. If only they would turn to Me and seek My face. Lift all your concerns to Me. Sit at My feet and offer your petitions. Tell Me all of your needs and concerns. Then, just as a child, totally trust Me to care for each need individually and with great care. Begin to praise Me for the answers, before you begin to see the results!

———

"I tell you the truth, unless you change and become like little children, you will never enter the kingdom of heaven. Therefore, whoever humbles himself like this child is the greatest in the kingdom of heaven. And, whoever welcomes a little child like this in my name, welcomes me." (Matthew 18:3-5)

Persevere

My Precious One,

The battle is raging and yet it has just begun. Set your eyes upon Me. You will learn to feel the calm in the storm. My children are under attack. You must persevere. You are being tested in this, but your countenance will remain pure. My love will pour forth from you unconditionally and you will reap the rewards. You are changing and forming lives while yours is changing and forming as well. Persevere. Remain in My presence and in My peace.

In time, you will see peace surround you, though others will only see chaos. Your job is to live and love unconditionally. Love and laughter will bring healing to My people. I have placed you as a ray of sunshine in the lives of many.. Trust Me completely, my child. I have placed you right where you are for many good reasons. You are touching lives. Lives will be changed and yours will be as well. I am in control. Show Me that you believe Me. Remain calm in all situations. Seek My direction. Step out in faith and believe that all is in My hands, now and forevermore.

Answering My Cries

My Precious One,

Your faithfulness to pray will be rewarded, for I hear your petitions and cry for help. Your prayers never fall on deaf ears. Know that I am constantly at work in your presence.

Find joy in Me, forevermore, for the day of the Lord is at hand. We have much to accomplish in a very short time! And My hand is on your life. Feel My presence.

At times, you say you know that I am present, but you must live on faith. Rest assured, I will never leave you or forsake you. I am constantly in your presence, wooing you by the power of My Holy Spirit that dwells within you.

Seek to know Me more intimately. It is a matter of learning to shut everything else out and taking up residence with Me and Me alone. The pain you suffer is a blessing, for it will allow you to come to Me in this intimate way. Do not shun it. It all serves its purpose and this too will mold you and refine you into the godly woman that I long for you to become. Do you not see how I am using your circumstances to mold and make you into that woman? Trust Me, totally and completely. This is the day the Lord has made, rejoice and be glad forevermore! Amen.

Praise Him Regardless

I turn randomly to Isaiah 42:10-13 and I read, "Song of Praise to the Lord!" Wow!

"Sing to the Lord a new song, his praise from the ends of the earth, you who go down to the sea, and all that is in it, you islands, and all who live in them . . . Let the people of Sela sing for joy; let them shout from the mountaintops. Let them give glory to the Lord and proclaim His praise in the islands. The Lord will march out like a mighty man, like a warrior he will stir up his zeal, with a shout he will raise the battle cry and will triumph over his enemies!"

M y Precious One,
Find nothing but joy in Me. Joy in your salvation. There is power, great power in praise and in thanksgiving.

When My people sing My praises and lift My name up in song, They are released by the power of My Holy Spirit to do great and mighty things that, in normal conditions, could not be accomplished. May joy fill your soul and may praises be forever on your lips, that My power may surge through you like an electrical current giving power to your mind, body, and soul. You must remain plugged into the source of your power by acknowledging My presence at all times and in all places. Set your eyes upon Me like flint. Do not take them off for a second for then you will become vulnerable to fall.

The longer you have remained in My presence, the more you will see this power that I am offering up to you. Find joy in Me, no matter how difficult the circumstances. The praise you offer Me should never be contingent on your circumstances. You must walk with Me freely, praising at all times and in all places. Joy, joy, joy . . . now and forever.

Warnings

I open my Bible and read: "The Lord said to Moses, 'How long will these people treat me with contempt? How long will they refuse to believe in me, in spite of all the miraculous signs I have performed among them?'" (Numbers 14:11)

My Precious One,

My children continue to walk down their own road, choosing to stop only occasionally to acknowledge My presence. What they need to do is fall prostrate before Me, confess their sins and, in repentance, worship Me.

Sadly, they think that token acknowledgments will satisfy My requirements for living a good life—that it will earn them a place in Heaven when they die. My child, tell them they are wrong! They continue in their selfish ways and turn their face from Mine. They choose not to acknowledge Me in their daily tasks. They think they can get along just fine in their own strength. However, they are testing Me, and in time I will be required to test them.

My child, I have called you to warn them ahead of time. Look for the opportunity, for the time is coming when you will speak again and they will listen; their eyes will be opened to receive My truth. Pray in the Spirit. Pray without ceasing. Set your eyes upon Me. Do all things through Christ who gives you strength, now and forevermore. Amen.

Pray for Hearts to be Softened

I turn to Isaiah and meditate on the Word:

Isaiah 43—God is my Savior.

43:12—He has revealed, saved, and proclaimed.

43:25—He who blots out my transgression, for my own sake and remembers my sins no more.

44:3—He will pour out His Spirit on my offspring. And His blessings on my descendants.

44:4—They will spring up like grass in a meadow, like poplar trees by flowing streams.

God does it all, but, we are to pray. Prayer is our responsibility. I know the prayers of the righteous are powerful and effective. (James 5:16).

I turn to Acts 26, the story of Paul's conversion. I see again, that it is only by God's grace that we are saved. God appointed Paul to be a witness and a servant. (verse 16). And, Paul was obedient to the vision God gave him (verse 19).

My Precious One,
Look to Me for all things. Seek My face to receive guidance for everything in your life. I will take you down the path of righteousness. I will lead you to the point of salvation. It is by the guidance of My Holy Spirit and My Holy Spirit alone that one is saved.

Pray for My Holy Spirit to speak to people's hearts. Pray that their hearts are softened, that seeds may be planted in soft, moist soil, that will allow the seed to take root and grow quickly to maturity. The days are evil and hearts are growing harder. Only the prayers of My people will prepare the soil to receive My seed. Even My children, My own children, are growing a hardened heart. They have accepted Me but they choose to stop there—they go no further. They do not seek My Word, and they see it all as too much time-consuming work.

Pray for My children; they need Me! They need My Word! They need to be able to hear and receive the instruction of My Holy Spirit. Only through prayer, your prayers, will they turn from their wicked ways and fall upon their knees and confess their sins. Pray without ceasing. Pray in the Spirit. Pray now and forever. Amen.

Seek Me First

My Precious One,

Joy in Me. Joy in your salvation. The day of the Lord is at hand! Confess your sins before the Father and acknowledge your wrongdoing. Fall prostrate before Me and seek My forgiveness. You must come to Me with a repentant heart, and you must seek Me and Me alone.

Life is filled with opportunities to follow other idols, but you must learn to recognize them and turn from them. It is in seeking Me and seeking Me alone that you will be freed to receive the richness of My Kingdom. My blessings far outweigh the momentary satisfaction you may receive from seeking and following after worldly idols.

Set your eyes upon heavenly sights. There is so much more for My children, if only they will look up! See things through spiritual eyes, rather than through earthly vision. It is too narrow and is often deceiving. Look into My face and feel the glory surround you. Take your hand off the comforts of the world. Remind yourself to keep your vision broad. Read My Word and you will find Me. Speak to Me in praise and prayer, and My glory will fall upon you.

My Gifts to You

My Precious One,

Open up your heart to Me and receive all that I long to give you. Just as a father longs to shower his child with gifts, I too, long to shower you with My blessings. However, you must receive them and not turn your back from them and walk away.

Many of My children choose to turn their back and walk away from the gifts I long to give them. They choose to accept some and reject others. They pick and choose! Can you imagine rejecting gifts given to you on your birthday or Christmas? Of course not! And yet, My children daily reject My gifts—the very gifts that would empower them to live a full and godly life.

You say, "I am rich; I have acquired wealth and do not need a thing!" I counsel you to buy from me gold refined in the fire, so you can become rich; and white clothes to wear, so you can cover your shameful nakedness; and salve to put on your eyes, so you can see" (Revelation 3:18).

The Word

My Precious One;
My book is a precious love letter written with carefully planned instructions to lead, guide, and direct you. Every word that came from the mouth of your Lord is recorded in the pages of this written document. It is a book of carefully planned instructions, given to My children to help them live a godly, reverent life. It is a book of love that will shower you with comfort and encouragement and peace for daily living. It is a two-edged sword that will speak to the very core of your heart. It brings peace, but it also causes turmoil. It brings to light the sin in your life. It points out the need to repent. It sheds light

on the good and on the evil. It speaks truth and reveals truth, even in the dark. It brings to light all truth, for truth must reign superior.

My children need to read My Word and study it and meditate on it. They must absorb the truths of My Word and act upon them, so they may be guided by the Spirit. My Word and My child will become one with Me, unified in the Spirit of the living God. Amen.

Joy Is the Answer

I read in 2 Corinthians 7 about the apostle Paul's joy:

7:1—Since we have these promises, dear friends, let us purify ourselves from everything that contaminates body and spirit, perfecting holiness out of reverence for God.

4b—I am greatly encouraged, in all our troubles, my joy knows no bounds.

5—For when we came into Macedonia, this body of ours had no rest, but we were harassed at every turn—conflicts on the outside, fears within.

6—But God, who comforts the downcast, comforted us.

8—Even if I caused you sorrow by my letter, I do not regret it. Though I did regret it—I see that my letter hurt you, but only for a little while . . .

9—yet now I am happy, not because you were made sorry, but because your sorrow led you to repentance. For you became sorrowful as God intended and so you were not harmed in any way by us.

10—Godly sorrow brings repentance that leads to salvation and leaves no regret but worldly sorrow brings death.

11—See what this godly sorrow has produced in you: what earnestness, what eagerness to clear yourselves, what indignation, what alarm, what longing, what concern, what readiness to see justice done.

My Precious One,

All you experience is a part of My plan. Do not be discouraged or disheartened. Do not allow circumstances to drag you down. You have surrendered your all to Me so rest in My everlasting arms, believing that all things work together for good for those who love Me.

Joy is the medicine that you need. Sing praises to My name and the praise will be like a healing salve, like the balm of Gilead. It will pour like a warm oil over your head, down over your entire being, bringing peace to your soul. All is well, My child. Trust in Me for all things. Rest in Me; be anxious for nothing.

By prayer and supplication, with thanksgiving in your heart, let all requests be known to God and peace will keep your heart and mind in Christ Jesus. Joy in Me! Joy in your salvation. The day of the Lord is at hand. Rest assured, I am with You. I am Your companion, your friend, your guide, and your confidant. You have no reason to fear anything at all, for all is well in My hands. Do you trust Me? Completely? Step out in faith and rejoice, no matter what your circumstances.

Waiting Again

My Precious One,

All is well, all is in My hands. Rest in My everlasting arms, trusting Me to provide for all of your needs and the needs of your loved ones. They too, are in My care. Allow My peace to permeate your entire being.

You must learn to yield your all to Me. You must learn to rest in My presence alone. As you learn to rest, you learn to wait upon Me. In resting and in waiting will be your strength.

You feel like you are on hold, now doing little to serve My Kingdom. Learn to recognize the benefits of waiting, watching, and resting. This is the time when you should set your eyes upon Me, rest in My goodness. Draw strength from Me so you will be rejuvenated and ready when I call you back into service. The joy of the Lord will be your strength.

You will be prepared and waiting to serve if you spend this time wisely: listening, learning, and writing. I have much to teach you and I have your undivided attention in the early morning hours. You are open and free to receive My word and incapable of interjecting your own thoughts.

The words I give to you are often not words for you alone. The time will come when you will share them with many. Rest assured that I will determine the time and place. Do not choose to go off on your own and make your own plans for them or your words will not be received.

Some will not receive the words I have spoken. Never look for man's approval. Look only to Me and you will never be disappointed. I know and see all. Trust in Me totally and completely. I have a perfect plan and you are a part of it. It is just now beginning to unfold.

Be forewarned that even the waiting time is a part of My plan. A far more important part of My plan is that "they that wait upon the Lord shall renew their strength. They shall mount up with wings of eagles. They shall run and not grow weary. They shall walk and not faint" (Isaiah 40:31).

Teach me, Lord, teach me, Lord, to wait. Amen.

Relinquish All

"But our citizenship is in heaven. And we eagerly await a Savior, from there, the Lord, Jesus Christ." (Philippians 3:20)

Recently, someone said that we don't know when Christ will return, so we must live each day expecting Him. We need to go on living as usual. This biblical perspective is the one I want to follow. Jesus could return today. Will I be ready? My Gramma Ross lived her life ready for Jesus to return. I want to live my life with daily expectation too.

Oh, Lord, fill my heart with eagerness of anticipation. I long to serve you and you alone. Amen.

My Precious One,
Look to Me for all things. You must not forsake Me! You know I will never leave you or forsake you, but can you say the same? Set your eyes upon Me. Look to Me in every circumstance. Do

not ever become overly burdened in a situation but instead turn to me immediately in prayer. I am always there. I am always ready to give advice.

When things become difficult and look overwhelming to you, seek My face. I will lead and guide you. I will carry the burden for you if you will allow. Relinquish all to Me. ALL! You can hand it over to the Master and walk away from it like a child who gives his mother the responsibility to complete a task that is too difficult for him. He hands it over and walks off to play, carefree and unconcerned about the results, because he knows it will all be better.

Leave your burdens at My feet. Do not carry them yourself. They will weigh you down until your vision is blocked from seeing Me. Turn loose your cares and concerns. I am the Almighty One, capable of all things. Rest in My care, in My everlasting arms, in the shadow of the Almighty, trusting me totally and completely to care for your every need. Joy.

———

"But seek first His kingdom and His righteousness, and all of these things will be given to you as well." (Matthew 6:33)

"For the lamb at the center of the throne will be their shepherd; He will lead them to springs of living water. and God will wipe away every tear from their eyes." (Revelation 7:17)

Refinement

My Precious One,

A new day is dawning, a new day is beginning. Rejoice, for there will be new opportunities and new challenges. This day will be like no other. "The LORD *has done it this very day; let us rejoice today and be glad" (Psalm 118:24).*

Look at each challenge, each situation as a lesson from Me, put there to refine, remold, and remake you into the perfect specimen that I created. Like clay upon a potter's wheel, I will do what it takes (allow what it requires) to form you into the perfect vessel that will hold the "living water." At times, you will feel out of shape, cracked and leaking, but I will add more living water to the clay that I might smooth and fix and remold you to be exactly what I long for you to be.

Trust Me completely. I am the perfect potter. Rest in My hands, trusting Me to mold you. If you rest in Me even in the midst of the refining it will be so much easier on you. When you yield to my corrections, the refining process will be accomplished so much more smoothly. By yielding your all to Me, I can form you with ease. It is when you resist that My job is made so much more difficult and you feel far greater pain.

So, rejoice in your trials and your tribulations, knowing that I, your Father God, am in charge. Rest quietly, relaxed in My everlasting arms. The presence of My Holy Spirit will surround you, and you will feel the glory of the Lord all about you. Trust Me. Trust me totally and completely. I am your Father God. As a little child that trusts his or her daddy without question, place your hand in Mine and walk with Me, knowing that I would never lead you astray.

We will walk this path of life together only if you choose to. It is your choice. I have already made Mine. I made it when I created you. I made it when I chose you before you were created in your mother's womb.

How about you? Will you choose Me? Daily? Reach out. Place your hand in Mine. Let us walk this journey together. "Two are better than one" (Ecclesiastes 4:9-12).

"His divine power has given us everything we need for life and godliness through our knowledge of Him who called us by His own glory and goodness. Through these He has given us His very great and precious promises, so that through them you may participate in the divine nature and escape the corruption in the world caused by evil desires. For this very reason, make every effort to add to your faith goodness; and to goodness, knowledge; and to knowledge, self-control; and to self control, perseverance; and to perseverance, godliness; and to godliness, brotherly kindness; and to brotherly kindness, love. For if you possess these qualities in increasing measure, they will keep you from being ineffective and unproductive in your knowledge of our Lord Jesus Christ. But if anyone does not have them, he is near-sighted and blind, and has forgotten that he has been cleansed from his past sins. Therefore, my brothers, be all the more eager to make your calling and election sure. For if you do these things, you will never fail, and you will receive a rich welcome into the eternal kingdom of our Lord and Savior Jesus Christ. Above all, you must

understand that no prophecy of scripture came about by the prophet's own interpretation. For prophecy never had its origin in the will of man, but men spoke from God as they were carried along by the Holy Spirit." (2 Peter 1:3-11, 20-21)

Fear

I awake from a deep sleep, singing "How Beautiful." Then I hear a man's voice. My windows are open. Fear runs right through me. I claim the power and protection of the blood of Jesus over myself and my house and cover myself in the armor of God.

I am fighting distraction. I am wide awake now; PTL (praise the Lord) for that. It seems more like it could have been my son talking in his sleep but I feel so vulnerable.

I don't want to feel like I can't leave my windows open. I decide to turn to God's Word. I turn to Jude 1:20 "But you, dear friends, build yourselves up in your most holy faith and pray in the Holy Spirit . . ."

I begin to pray in the Spirit after I write the words below. When I first read it, I am too stunned to even see that there are instructions for me. Why don't I remember to always pray in the Spirit when I am anxious? It always brings a peace and calm to me.

We must remember to "keep ourselves in God's love as we wait for the mercy of our Lord Jesus Christ to bring us to eternal life." We must "be merciful to those who doubt, snatch others from the fire and save them; to others show mercy, mixed with fear, hating even the clothing stained by corrupted flesh." We need to persevere, because, ". . . in the last days scoffers will come, scoffing and following their own evil desires" (2 Peter 3:3).

*M*y *Precious One,*
Do not fear, for man can do nothing to you that I do not allow. But be alert. Be watchful. Not everyone is a friend but some come as wolf in sheep's clothing. You must pray for more wisdom and more discernment. I will then reveal much more to you.

Prepare your heart to receive, for the road is not easy and the journey can be tiring. Look not to man, but look to Me. I will open up your eyes and reveal truth to you, some of which will be very difficult to receive, but if you remain focused, you will see things through spiritual eyes. Much will be revealed to you in a mighty and glorious way of revelation, knowledge that is only imparted to my most faithful.

Again, I have chosen you. The question is will you choose Me? Will you choose My way even though My path will provide some hardship and some pain? Remember that following the pain comes the blessings of My truth only revealed to My most faithful.

Will you choose to join the faithful? To continue on your present path? To join in on the long journey that will eventually bring you face to face with your Father God and your Creator? The time is now. The time is short. There is no turning back for My faithful ones. We must press on towards the mark. We must persevere until the end at which time God will rule all and we will reign in the glorious Kingdom of God, forever and ever. Amen.

Rest

"Be patient, then, brothers and sisters, until the Lord's coming. See how the farmer waits for the land to yield its valuable crop, patiently waiting for the autumn and spring rains. You too, be patient and stand firm, because the Lord's coming is near. Don't grumble against one another, brothers and sisters, or you will be judged. The Judge is standing at the door!

Brothers and sisters, as an example of patience in the face of suffering, take the prophets who spoke in the name of the Lord. As you know, we count as blessed those who have persevered. You have heard of Job's perseverance and have seen what the Lord finally brought about. The Lord is full of compassion and mercy." (James 5:7-11)

Oh Lord, give me the faith to receive your healing upon my body. I long to receive all that you have for me, Lord!

My Precious One,
Lift your eyes to the hills for where does your help come from? From the Lord who made the heavens and the earth?

Look into His face. Feel His arms surround you. Feel His comfort and His grace. Rejoice. Today is the day the Lord has made. Rejoice and be glad in it. The day of the Lord is at hand.

Rest quietly in Me. Stop your rushing and reflect. Rushing and hurrying just weary the body. Your body is the vessel of the Holy Spirit within you. You are not your own. You were bought with a price, so glorify God in your body.

Rejoice, for the day of the Lord is at hand and all is in My hands. Relinquish all to Me. Do not hold back. Rest assured that I am in control. Fret not, because all is a part of My divine plan. I leave nothing to unfold. I am who I am. See how your controlling spirit tires you when you try to do My work without My guidance. See how the effort increases when you do not freely yield to My ways. Your intentions are usually good, even spiritual, but you must yield to Me or eventually frustration sets in because your plans do not come to completion and oh, the time wasted even grieves Me.

Rest in My everlasting arms. Joy in My presence. Forget your anxieties and rest in My peace knowing I, your Father God, truly am in charge. Let My peace permeate your entire being. Let me soothe your aches and pains. Today is a new day and a new beginning. Rest quietly in My presence and receive My healing power, now and forever more. Rest, rest in Me.

———

"Make every effort to enter through the narrow door, because many, I tell you will try to enter and will not be able to do so . . . People will come from east and west and north and south, and will take their places at the feast in the kingdom of God. Indeed there are those who are last who will be first, and first who will be last." (Luke 13:24, 29-30)

Look Beyond Your Circumstances

My Precious One,

The journey is long and often difficult. You may choose an easier path if you like, but the blessings you receive will be in proportion to your choosing. I continue to protect you at your request but, you also must not, I repeat, must not, look at the circumstances and the way they appear.

When you view life through spiritual eyes the picture is quite different. It doesn't look the same at all. You must see the total picture to receive the proper view. I am doing a great and mighty work. Man's vision is too limited to receive the whole plan. Through spiritual eyes the plan can be revealed to you over time. You cannot take it in all at one time. Trust me; remember to look beyond the circumstances.

Rejoice at All Times!

My Precious One,

Your body is weak and you feel fatigue. Rest in My arms and trust Me to heal you. Be filled with My joy in the midst of your pain. Know that I am in control. Joy, joy in Me alone. You must learn this secret of My Kingdom: to rejoice at all times. Lift up to Me a sacrifice of praise. Put a song on your lips and sing from your heart. Do it even though you do not feel like it, rejoicing in Me rather than your circumstances.

I am the only real stability in your life. I am the Alpha and the Omega. I am the beginning and the end. I never change and I never leave you . Lift your burdens to Me. Cast your anxiety upon Me. I will care for you and your loved ones. There is nothing too great for Me to handle but first you must lay it all down at My feet and not pick it back up again. You must learn to trust Me to care for every detail in your life while communing with Me in prayer, praise, and thanksgiving.

Be filled with My joy, even in the midst of your difficult circumstances. Even when things are seemingly out of your control, rejoice, rejoice in Me and in Me alone. When you learn to rise above your circumstances and look at Me, instead of the problem, your joy will be made full.

Strive to look at Me. Strive to look up, over, above, and beyond all things. I will carry you, not just the burden, but you. Allow Me to carry you. Rest your head against My breast. Feel My arms surround you and your mind, body, soul, and spirit. I will heal all of you if only you can learn to rest in Me. Stop your striving and give up. Give it all up! Now and forever more. Amen.

No Worries

I turn to Isaiah 42: "Song of Praise to the Lord," and this is what jumps off the page . . .

Psalm 42:10-12: "Sing to the Lord a new song, his praise from the ends of the earth . . . sing for joy, shout from the mountaintops; let them give glory to the Lord and proclaim His praise in the islands."

Then I turn to Matthew 6:25: DO NOT WORRY . . . (vs. 27) "Who of you by worrying can add a single hour to his life?" Amen!

Suffering and Compassion

Without the sword and suffering there is no cross to bear. I awake, (sort of) thinking of Moses. He couldn't enter the Promised Land without suffering. I too, must suffer if I want to enter the promised land and receive God's blessings.

Suffering brings meaning to God's blessings. We have to pay the price to appreciate what God has given us or will give us. We are like spoiled children. When we are given everything and don't have to pay a price for it, we don't appreciate its full value. Suffering produces appreciation, therefore, we should never shun suffering for ourselves or for anyone else.

My Precious One,
Your joy will be made full in Me. The joy of your salvation will fill your soul and reach out and encompass those who surround you. Be filled with My compassion. Reach out and touch those around you. Allow your heart to melt in their presence, showing them My love for them. Many will not understand but your constant and forgiving love will become a testimony of My love for them. Reach out and touch. Bring comfort to those who hurt.

I have given you this compassion for a reason. Use it for My glory. Look at others through your spiritual eyes. See them as I see them: broken, lost, little sheep that need a Master to carry them, a Shepherd to lead them.

Even the stubborn ones are crying out. They cry out louder in a more rebellious way. Many turn and run because of their anger and accusations. I tell you, their pain is greater and their need for love deeper. Do not turn your back. Reach out in gentleness. Do not grow weary in doing good. Your reward will be tenfold in heaven.

Trust Me to provide the compassion needed. Your joy will be full and your cup will run over into the saucer and the wounded will be healed. Trust Me for all things. Joy in your suffering and in suffering for others who are in pain. It is a jewel of My Kingdom.

One day, you will really understand, for you share in My cup, in My cup of pain. You will one day see how sharing this with Me here on Earth will bring tremendous blessing one day in the heavenlies when you enter the holy of holies and stand in My presence for eternity. Joy. Joy in all things, now and forevermore. Amen.

Keep Your Eyes on Him

My Precious One,
Your joy will be made full. You are in the midst of the battle and it is impossible to see the end in sight at this point. But, you must learn to lift your eyes up to the Lord, the one who made the heavens and the earth. If you look only at your circumstances at this moment you will be crushed.

Persevere and go on. You must not look back but look ahead. Keep your goal in mind and then move forward in baby steps, one step at a time. Trust Me completely. Hold onto My promises. Speak them from the roof tops. Do not speak curses on yourself or your children or on anyone else. Speak My word and hold fast to it, that it might infiltrate your entire being and overtake you. It is by My sword that you will overcome.

"Sword"—Wow! God's Word is our sword. This is no coincidence. This just blows me away. I wonder how many people have seen this. I pray for a **word** from the s**word**. In my mind, I think, *Isaiah 53*. I randomly open to the exact page: Isaiah 53:11, "After the suffering of his soul, he will see the light of life, and be satisfied, by his knowledge my righteous servant will justify many, and he will bear their iniquities."

I hear . . .

Andrea is suffering now—but she will see the light of life! Jesus Christ will save her, and she will no longer be dissatisfied with life. She will be righteous. She will be wise. She will see truth and the truth will set her free.

"Do not be afraid; you will not suffer shame. Do not fear disgrace; you will not be humiliated" (Isaiah 54:4). You will forget the shame of your youth and remember no more the reproach of your widowhood. (That's me; thank you, Lord!) *"For your maker is your husband, The Lord Almighty, is His name—the Holy one of Israel is your redeemer; He is called the God of all the earth. The Lord will call you back as if you were a wife deserted and distressed in spirit,—a wife who married young, only to be rejected, says your God. For a brief moment I abandoned you, but with deep compassion I will bring you back. I hid my face from you for a moment,*

but with everlasting kindness I will have compassion on you, says the Lord your Redeemer" (Isaiah 54:5-8).

Look to Him

My Precious One,

Take joy now in this present day of suffering, for in times to come your joy will be even far greater. You must learn to look at life through spiritual eyes, keeping them on the finish, the end of the course. Do not look at the obstacles along the way or they will make you stumble and fall. Then you will not be able to pick yourself up but instead will remain down and deflated.

Keep your vision up. Lift it higher. Seek to see the end result, not the present and difficult circumstance. Today is a new day and a new beginning. Set your focus on Me, your Father God and do not take your eyes from Me. The journey may seem long and difficult, but, if you look to Me and do not stray, all will be well with your soul.

———

"For you were once darkness, but now you are light in the Lord. Live as children of light (for the fruit of the light consists in all goodness, righteousness and truth,) and find out what pleases the Lord. Have nothing to do with the fruitless deeds of darkness, but rather expose them. For it is shameful even to mention what the disobedient do in secret. But everything exposed by the light becomes visible." (Ephesians 5:8-13)

"Do everything without complaining or arguing, so that you may become blameless and pure, children of God without fault in a crooked and depraved generation, in which you shine like stars in the universe." (Philippians 2:14)

Die to Self

My Precious One,

Life is a series of steps, a progression of lessons. No one escapes them. They just move along at different paths. Some people are more stubborn and their way seems more difficult while others are more complacent or fear pain more so that they go along with the plan with less resistance. My children are unique and no two fit into one mold, though all must ultimately come to know their Creator, their Maker. All must learn to bow in reverence to Me and learn to worship and adore Me. Some never do.

My heart breaks for those who find it eternally difficult to find Me. Self is a powerful inhibitor. It prevents many from surrendering their all to their Creator, the Almighty, their Father God. Die daily to self. Recognize self for what it is and learn to daily surrender, daily. If you wait longer it becomes increasingly difficult to give your all to Me. Self intertwines like a web that grips and holds firm to the selfish desires of your will. It prevents one from releasing and relinquishing the self desires for my will.

Seek My will. In order to seek it, you must remain in a state of constant communion with Me through prayer. Seek My presence. Look into My face and listen to My voice speak truths to you; then take action and do as I have called you. Do not step back but go forward, seeking to walk in My ways and fulfill My divine will for thy life.

I am your Father God and I truly know what is best for you. You must trust Me totally and completely, walking in My ways, holding My hand and serving Me along the way. Do not hold back in fear. Fear is not of Me. Be washed in My blood, loved and protected, because of your trust in Me and your faithfulness to follow me now and forever more. Amen.

———

"What I tell you in the dark, speak in the daylight; what is whispered in your ear, proclaim from the roofs. Do not be afraid of those who kill the body but cannot kill the soul. Rather, be afraid of the One who can destroy both soul and body in hell." (Matthew 10:27)

"Therefore go and make disciples of all nations, baptizing them in the name of the Father and of the Son and of the Holy Spirit, and teaching them to obey everything I have commanded you. And surely I am with you always, to the very end of the age." (Matthew 28:19-20)

Fasting

My Precious One,
You are not alone for I am with you unto the ends of the earth. Fasting will draw you nearer to Me and make you more

attune to the spiritual. The self does die and become more subservient to Me, to the spiritual side of things. It changes your focus from the world to the heavenlies. It is a purifying process of body, mind, and spirit. Joy in the fact that it is a tool I have given you to overcome the flesh. It sharpens your vision and draws you closer into My presence. You then can hear My voice more clearly as I speak to you.

When you become dull to spiritual things, fasting is the key to bring you back into My presence. It is the world that pulls and tugs for your affections. You draw away slowly, subtly, often without any realization that it is occurring.

Joy in Me. Joy in your salvation, for the day of the Lord is at hand. Spend time in prayer and fasting for your loved ones. There is great power in this combination. Do not lose sight of it. It is a mystery to many—a tool to be used by My children to accomplish the seemingly impossible. Joy. Joy in Me.

―――

"The Lord said, 'Go out and stand on the mountain in the presence of the Lord, for the Lord is about to pass by.'" (1 Kings 19:11)

"Be still, and know that I am God; I will be exalted among the nations, I will be exalted in the earth. The Lord almighty is with us; the God of Jacob is our fortress." (Psalm 46:10)

"God is our refuge and strength, an ever-present help in trouble." (Psalm 46:1)

Surrender All

*M**y Precious One,***

Your joy will be complete when you truly learn to give up your all for Me. When you learn to truly, totally, and completely trust in Me. When you learn to set aside anxious thoughts and really know that I am in charge of all things. When you learn to surrender your will for mine in every area of thy life. Then and only then will you truly experience the joy of the Lord.

Life is a process. A series of steps. It is leading you to this point of trust, this realization of my presence, this attitude of surrender. It is not an easy road but the more you rely on Me the easier it will be. Fellowship with Me, cry out to Me, and I will answer.

I long to commune with you, My child. I long to spend time with all of My children, just as you enjoy being with your children when they are loving and agreeable. I too long for those times.

But, do you shun them when they are in distress or anxious? No, you too, even in their humanness and selfishness, go to their rescue. Can you not see how far greater is my love for you? Though at times your flesh causes you to want to reject your child, I will never reject you. I long for you to know this. I long for you to understand the love I have for you. It is a deep, everlasting, affectionate love that really is humanly impossible to totally understand. But, through spiritual eyes you can receive it.

Seek to receive it by spending time with Me. Draw apart from your worldly responsibilities. The more time you spend with Me, the more time you will find to do the necessary mundane things of the world. Look to Me and I will supply all of your needs now and forevermore. Amen.

———

"I am the good shepherd. The good shepherd lays down his life for the sheep."(John 10:11)

". . . Our God will fight for us." (Nehemiah 4:20)

"I am the good shepherd; I know my sheep and my sheep know me . . . My sheep listen to my voice; I know them, and they follow me."(" (John 10:14, 27)

The Sword of God's Word

My Precious One,
Your life is in My hands. Rest quietly in Me and know that no one can touch your soul. Your body can be abused and harmed and the enemy can come against you with accusations and try to break you down in spirit and in truth, but if you know My Word, the Word will set you free. Read it. Study it. Absorb it. Hold it close to your heart. Allow it to permeate your entire being, for it is like a two-edged sword that will bring you peace and at the same time cut through the lies of those who try to harm you.

It will shed light on untruths and bring to light the truth. It is a sword. You must carry it into battle. You must not drop it or set it down or you will become defenseless. It is your tool in every battle. Take care of it. Shine it. Sharpen it. Protect it, so that when the battle begins again you will be ready. You will be prepared. Hold fast to your word. Speak it silently to give you strength, holding fast to the promises that I have given you.

Listen to My voice speak them to you. At times I will reveal truth to you and ask you to speak it aloud. Listen carefully so you will not miss My instruction. It must be used carefully and only at the appropriate time. Learn to be obedient. I am your Master and your Commander in battle. I long to protect your life even to death.

If you remain independent of Me, you will not survive. Rest in the confidence that I care deeply for you and I long to protect you. Seek My face, especially in the midst of the battle. I am always here for you. I will never leave you or never forsake you. But, you must acknowledge My presence to receive the full benefit of My protection.

Look into My face. Listen to My voice and obey My commands. For I will be with you to the ends of the earth, now and forevermore. Amen.

Total Dependence on Christ

(Written in my school closet)

My Precious One,
Enter into My presence with thanksgiving in your heart. Enter My courts with praise. You are being allowed to see the hurt

and pain in this world through the pains of your students. Their emotional needs are so great that you cannot meet them. Their needs keep them from receiving the teaching you have to offer them. Then a wall builds and neither of you can function.

This is a smaller picture of the bigger world. Everything is shutting down. The needs of people are so great that they cannot meet their own needs, let alone others. No one has anyone to save them but Me. The world has come to a place where they have no one to turn to. This is the only way they will call out to Me. Even you will find that total dependence on Me will be your only answer.

You will learn to rest in My everlasting arms. You will learn to abide in My love. Do not turn your frustration inward and harbor anger and resentment. Do not turn your frustrations outward and take them out on others. Lift them upward, for I am ready to receive them. Rise above them. This is why I speak to you. I will teach you to look at your circumstances through your spiritual eyes and you will come to understand that which is taking place in these end times. They are not easy nor will it get any easier. Do not look at the circumstances. Look to Me and to Me alone.

"When evening comes you say, 'It will be fair weather, for the sky is red' and in the morning, 'Today it will be stormy, for the sky is red and overcast.' You know how to interpret the appearance of the sky, but you cannot interpret the signs of the times." (Matthew 16:2)

The end times are here.

Life Is a Journey to God

My Precious One,

All of life has its purpose . . . from life to death. It is a journey one takes to come to know their heavenly Father, to prepare them for life eternal. It is a process of steps upward or downward, the choice being yours here on earth. Of course, you may take some steps upward followed by downward steps but in the end you will reach the destination of your choice. The hurts and pains that you must suffer help to chart your course. You choose to either run to Me for comfort or run away from Me in anger.

All is part of the process to refine you, mold you, and make you into the person I long for you to become, but you have the freedom to choose the way in which you will go. See life as a journey, as a challenge. Meet life's difficulties with eager anticipation of overcoming. I can provide all that you need, you only must choose to ask. Choose to seek Me. Choose to look past the present circumstances and see where the challenges can take you. Your attitude can make all of the difference. Your joy can be made full in the most difficult of circumstances when you learn to look past them and learn to anticipate the results. Joy. Joy in Me, forevermore, for I have your best interests in mind as always.

———

"The sting of death is sin, and the power of sin is the law. But thanks be to God! He gives us the victory through our Lord, Jesus Christ."
(1 Corinthians 15:56-57)

"So whether you eat or drink or whatever you do, do it all for the glory of God" (1 Corinthians 10:31)

". . . he will not let you be tempted beyond what you can bear. But when you are tempted, he will also provide a way out so that you can endure it." (1 Corinthians 10:31)

———

Then I turn to Proverbs and see: "Whoever rebukes a person will in the end gain favor rather than one who has a flattering tongue" (Proverbs 28:23) . . . and I think of my daughter and me. Then I think of my past students, the ones I was so tough with and how they always come back to visit me, and I remember that "every word of God is flawless; he is a shield to those who take refuge in him" (Proverbs 30:5).

"See, the former things have taken place, and new things I declare; before they spring into being I announce them to you." (Isaiah 42:9)

Your God-Given Emotions

My Precious One,
Joy in Me. Joy in your salvation, for the day of the Lord is at hand. Feel My presence surround you. Feel My angels round about you. Know of My comforting power and of My grace. I will restore your joy. I will diminish your anger.

Your emotions are God-given. They are a part of you as well as a part of Me. I have given them to you as a release from that which you experience. You need to learn to express them in a Godly manner. They are there for you, to enhance your quality of life. They are there to help you, but are capable of destroying you, if you do not express them appropriately.

Expressing your emotions can be healing. Bottling them up can be destructive. Learn to live freely in Me. I, your Father God, care for you so deeply. I long for you to be free in Me to joy in your salvation but to also freely express your hurt, anger and pain. All is a beautiful part of what makes up you. Learn to rest quietly in Me knowing that I, your Father God, care so deeply for you that I have planned even every avenue of escape for you.

If only you will take this to heart and really know that I am all that you need. I have already provided all that you need. ALL. It is at your disposal. Look to Me, my child. Look to Me. Set your eyes upon Me and know that all is well, no matter how things appear. All is well.

Quiet Time Moments

My Precious One,
Come to Me. Sit at My feet. Look into My face and eagerly anticipate a joyful communion time with me. I love to speak to you, to share with you, to commune with you. So many of My children miss out on this close and intimate time. In the hustle and bustle of daily living they find no time to draw apart. Their focus is on the

worldly tasks that engulf them. Each must make a concerted effort and it is often a struggle to maintain that personal time.

The enemy longs to distract you. Your strength and your power comes from Me. You cannot be re-energized unless you draw apart. So many of My children fail to recognize this and the less time they spend with Me, the less they desire to spend time with me. It is a spiral process that depletes and destroys. You must fight to maintain this intimate relationship. You must meet with Me even when it seems that you will struggle more with life responsibilities. Time with Me will allow you to accomplish all else in record time. Communion time with Me allows My Spirit to flow freely and allows Me to work in thy life in most amazing ways.

You have a choice. Choose to spend time with Me or not. I long to love you and be loved back. I long to share with you and have you share back. Together we will become one and the power and strength of My Kingdom will be magnified. So seek My face at all times and in all places but also choose to draw apart alone with Me, to commune with Me, to learn from Me. I will speak and you will listen. Then you will speak and I will listen. A deep, loving relationship will evolve and you will grow in grace and in stature as I prepare you for life in eternity with Me.

The Battle Rages

Father God, help! I am hiding in this closet, a retreat from battle. I have had arrows shot at me almost every minute of this day. I awoke joyful and longing to remain so after confessing my negative attitude last night. My day started with mud tracked across the carpet. I am exhausted and was at 10:00 this morning.

The children in class cannot sit still, or pay attention. They are like worms in hot ashes. I pray peace on them. Father, peace like a river needs to flow over, around and through them. Help me, Lord to be a source of peace for them. If I waited on them to all be still and quiet I would never finish anything but I feel like I am fighting a losing battle. The wiggles are winning. It is a miracle that they have learned anything at all! Help me, Lord. Teach me, Lord. I'm screaming out to you as my students scream out to me!

My Precious One,
You are being tested and you will overcome. There is great spiritual battle taking place in your classroom. You are not immune to it anywhere or at any time. You stood for Me yesterday. You spoke My name. You taught your children the meaning of Christmas.

Lives are being changed. Hearts are being touched. Go on, move forward. Be bold. Your prayers for that one special little boy are revealing truths that have been hidden. Continue to pray in the spirit for this young one. Others will come to you too. You must see your job from a spiritual view point. The teaching here is secondary. The spiritual needs to come first. This is new for you but the end times are here and my creation must know the truth. It is your job to share it, in spirit and in truth. I will reveal to you the how. Just stay ever so close to Me and your eyes will be opened up to see. Your vision will be widened and your discernment will increase.

Listen to Me, child, and do as I call you to do. Serve me. Rest in Me. Do not fear. I have a plan, a perfect plan, and you are an important part of that plan. Rest assured, know that I am God, Creator of ALL the earth. Sing praises to My name. Blessed be the name of the Lord and all else will come to pass in My perfect timing according to My perfect plan.

———

"Like a city whose walls are broken through is a person who lacks self-control." (Proverbs 25:28)

"Like a maniac shooting flaming arrows of death is one who deceives their neighbor and says, "I was only joking!" (Proverbs 26:18)

More Suffering

My Precious One,
Trials and tribulations have come your way to mold you and make you into the person I long for you to become. The way you suffer is part of My plan. I long for you to learn to rejoice in your sufferings. To take the pain in stride thus overcoming. All is a perfect part of My plan. Learn to rejoice in various trials in your life . . .

———

"Consider it pure joy, my brothers and sisters, whenever you face trials of many kinds, because you know that the testing of your faith produces perseverance. Let perseverance finish its work so that you may be mature and complete, not lacking anything. If any of you lacks wisdom, you should ask God, who gives generously to all without finding fault, and it will be given to you. But when you ask, you must believe and not doubt, because the one who doubts is like a wave of the sea, blown and tossed by the wind. That person should not expect to receive anything from the Lord. Such a person is double-minded and unstable in all they do." (James 1:2-8)

"But the wisdom that comes from heaven is first of all pure; then peace-loving, considerate, submissive, full of mercy and good fruit, impartial and sincere." (James 3:17)

Temptation

My Precious One,
You are not your own. You were bought with a price so glorify God in your body. All is mine and yet I give it to you. You must be disciplined and alert to temptation. Satan will try to come against you and weaken you in every area of your life just as Christ was tempted. Your close communion with Me will allow you to recognize Satan's attacks. You will be prepared to stand up and fight if only you are saturated in My word, in prayer and praise, the perfect tools for battle, to fight the evil ways of your enemy.

Do not hold back. Be bold. Bring the evil to light and face it full on. Do not hide or turn your back. Even though the glory is your rear guard, you must look into the face of evil with boldness, not defensively, but offensively. I have provided the necessary tools. All you must do is pick them up and use them. Go ahead in prayer and praise knowing that I am with you and knowing that the battle has already been won long ago, when My Son died upon the cross for your sins—yes, yours!

————

"'Be strong and courageous. Do not be afraid or discouraged because of the King of Assyria and the vast army with him, for there is a greater power with us than with him. With him is only the arm of flesh, but with us is the Lord our God to help us and to fight our battles.' And, the people gained confidence from what Hezekiah, the King of Judah, said."(2 Chronicles 32:7-8)

Endure Hardship as Discipline

My Precious One,
Oh my child, I am always there for you. You are precious in My sight. I hear your heart cry. I feel your soul pain. I know all that you are and all that you need. Rest assured in My everlasting arms. The burdens I bring to bear in your life are all there for a reason. They are there to teach you something, to mold you and make

you into the person I long for you to become. You must learn to lift your burdens to Me, to overcome and to rise above, for I will carry them all for you, but you must learn to turn them over to Me.

It is all a part of your growing process as you learn and achieve at higher levels of stability. I am near. I will never leave you or forsake you. Rest confidently in My presence in all situations. Allow Me to guide and to direct you now and eternally. All you experience here on earth has a purpose and all will help to prepare you for your life in eternity. Shun nothing that I bring into your life. Lift your heart to Me filled with praise and thanksgiving on every occasion and in every situation, now and forever more. Amen.

———

"I will lift my eyes to the hills—where does my help come from? My help comes from the Lord, the maker of heaven and earth. He will not let your foot slip—he who watches over you will not slumber; indeed, he who watches over Israel will not slumber nor sleep. The Lord watches over you—The Lord is your shade at your right hand; the sun will not harm you by day, nor the moon by night. The Lord will keep you from all harm—he will watch over your life; the Lord will watch over your coming and going, both now and forevermore." *(Psalm 121:1-8)*

More Discipline for Transformation

*M*y *Precious One,*

All in life happens for a reason. I am honing you and forming you into the bride, the body of Christ. The process is not easy, nor is it pleasant, but in the end you will shine like pure gold. It is all a process designed by Me, your Father God. Check yourself and do not let sin overtake you. Your selfish desires will try to shove Me out and overtake the spiritual. You must learn to depend totally and completely upon Me, your Father God.

Set your face like flint upon the goal of becoming Christlike, of being transformed into the likeness of Christ. I long for you to shine, to radiate the love of Christ to this dying world. To attain this you must suffer, and suffer you will. Through this refining process you will come to know Me and understand Me in a deep revelational manner. I long for you to know Me intimately. Do you long for it as well? Seek Me in prayer and in fasting and revelation knowledge will be revealed to you. Trust Me. Trust Me completely now and forevermore. Amen.

———

*"Make every effort to live in peace with everyone and to be holy; without holiness no one will see the Lord. See to it that no one falls short of the **grace of God** and that no bitter root grows up to cause trouble and defile many" (Hebrews 12:14-15, emphasis mine).*

*"Brothers and sisters, we do not want you to be uninformed about those who sleep in death, so that you do not grieve like the rest of mankind, **who have no hope**" (1 Thessalonians 4:13, emphasis mine).*

I think of friends grieving for my deceased husband David—hopelessness! I pray they will come to know the reality of Christ!

There is hope in situations that cause us to suffer. Our hope comes from the Lord who made the heavens and the earth. He will never leave us, never forsake us. He knows of our hurts and our pains for He too experienced it when here on Earth. Now He suffers again with us as we are one in mind, body, and soul.

"And my God will meet all of your needs according to His glorious riches in Christ Jesus" (Philippians 4:19). Everything we need is found in the person of Jesus Christ—everything. WOW!!

We need not ever worry!

Christmas/Rest

My Precious One,

Today is a new day and a new beginning—the birthday of the King of Kings and Lord of Lords. It is a call to the nations to fall upon their knees and worship Me.

Many miss the truth of the babe lying in the manger. Many do not see the reality of the King of Kings and Lord of Lords. They cannot see past the stable, past the manger. They look through worldly eyes and miss the whole point of My true existence. They do not know to look into My face, to draw strength from Me and to seek rebirth themselves.

Go out into the world and tell them. Do not miss an opportunity to share Me with others. Many are hungry and many are seeking. The void within their heart is so great and yet they do not know how to fill it. Tell them. Speak My truth. Open your eyes to see. Open your mouth and the words I give you will pour forth like a rushing waterfall, spilling over and consuming all in its path, taking over with a mighty power of the Holy Spirit, bringing some to their knees and knocking some over with the greatest of power, depending on their point of readiness and willingness to accept Me into their lives.

All this will happen because of My Holy Spirit. You must only be willing to be obedient to My calling, ready to do as I call you.. I have a mission for you! I know you long to serve Me, to teach and to speak that others might be saved. But, first you must learn to be content in your present circumstances. You must learn to wait upon the Lord, and not to rush ahead of the Holy Spirit but to be content even doing nothing.

First, you must learn to be content by just being, not doing. Learn to remain in My presence, quiet and still, doing nothing, saying nothing, planning nothing, just being. It is an important key to understanding Me fully and completely. And it is necessary before I can truly be released to work through you at all times and in all places. It is also a necessary key to restoring your strength following a battle, and is a trait needed before entering battle. Learn it now and great blessing will come your way. Learn to rest in My everlasting arms now and forever more. Amen.

Life Lessons

I came to believe years ago that everyone must experience certain things in their own life. Now I believe that if you don't experience some things personally that you will still experience them through those you love. We escape very little. Life here is preparation for life eternal.

My Precious One,
Life is a series of lessons. See it this way and eagerly anticipate the next. Not all will be free from pain for it is in pain and suffering that the greatest growth occurs. Learn to find joy in your pain by looking past the present circumstances and seeing that the end result will produce maturity and wisdom. Have hope in knowing that all is a part of My plan. By trusting Me and relinquishing all to Me, all will be well. All will be a blessing. Joy. Joy in Me. See My hand in every circumstance. Look for it. Grasp it. Hold on to it. Do not take your eyes from My face. When you turn to the circumstances instead, your hope will plummet and you will lose sight of My purpose. When this occurs, your faith dips and the joy dissipates. Hold on to Me, your Lord and your Savior, now and forevermore.

———

"The law of the Lord is perfect, refreshing the soul. The statutes of the Lord are trustworthy, making wise the simple. The precepts of the Lord are right, giving joy to the heart. The commands of the Lord are radiant, giving light to the eyes. The fear of the Lord is

pure, enduring forever. The decrees of the LORD are firm, and all of them are righteous. They are more precious than gold, than much pure gold; they are sweeter than honey, than honey from the honeycomb" (Psalm 19:7-10).

Life Events

My Precious One,

Life is a series of events laid out and prepared by Me, your Jehovah. All is in My perfect timing and in My perfect plan. When you can fully grasp this truth, you will find true peace and true joy.

You spend much time grumbling and complaining over the hardships in your life. If you will only choose to step back and see these difficult situations through spiritual eyes and realize the molding of your soul that is taking place, the frustration could be replaced with joyful anticipation of the future rather than fear. The root of your discomfort is fear—fear of not being able to accomplish the goals you've set out for yourself. The fear of failure. Even the fear of pain.

You long for your life to be perfect, full of joy and peace and free from pain. If only you could see that a life like that would make you soft and spoiled and self-centered, then you would rejoice more in your sufferings. It is in the difficult times that you draw nearer to Me; you seek My comfort and My guidance. It is in the difficult times that you seem more able to receive and accept My miracle working power.

Open up your eyes. Be willing to receive all that I bring into your life. Seek Me more in prayer. Do not become so focused on the problem that you become overwhelmed by the circumstances. When you take your eyes off of Me, you will drown into the depth of your problems, and only when you cry aloud to Me once again and reach out your hand from the depths of the sea will I be able to rescue you. It is by your will, by your choice, that I am allowed to pick you back up and set you on your feet. The only way you can maintain the joy and peace you so long for is to set your eyes on Me. Do not remove them for even a minute. You may fall again and again, but all you must do is speak My name and I will rescue you.

I never leave you. I never forsake you. It is you, as I've said before, that often chooses to leave Me. Seek to remain in My presence. Sing songs of praise. Lift up My name in worship and adoration. Cling to My Word, seeking me as you read it, My love letter written to you. Seek the gems and jewels I long to give you. They have already been offered. Choose to accept them by opening up my Word and reading. Drink it in like water when you are thirsty, for it will truly bring refreshment to your soul.

———

"At my first defense, no one came to my support, but everyone deserted me . . . But the Lord stood at my side and gave me strength, so that through me the message might be fully proclaimed and all the Gentiles might hear it. And I was delivered from the lion's mouth. The Lord will rescue me from every evil attack and will bring me safely to His heavenly kingdom. To Him be glory for ever and ever. Amen." (2 Timothy 4:16-18)

"The Son is the radiance of God's glory and the exact representation of his being, sustaining all things by his powerful word . . . Because he himself suffered when he was tempted, he is able to help those who are being tempted." (Hebrews 1:3, 2:18)

Stay Attuned

My Precious One,
Set your eyes upon Me and Me alone. If your focus is Me—drawing nearer to Me, listening to Me, seeking My Holy presence, worshiping Me, adoring Me—all else will fall into place. It is the job of My Holy Spirit to plan, prepare, and move you into action. Do not take over His job. Seek Me and Me alone and all else will be revealed to you in a very short time. In My presence, time passes quickly or slowly depending upon what you long for. Being in My presence is such a joy and a comfort that you become unaware of time. You can live this way moment to moment, more and more, as you become more attuned to Me, your Father God and your Creator. Joy. Joy in Me, now and forevermore. Amen.

I read in Acts 28 about how Paul shakes off a snake that should have killed him. He lays hands on a man and prays for his healing. He preaches God's Word from morning until evening: some believe, some do not. Boldly and without hindrance he preaches the Kingdom of God and teaches about the Lord Jesus Christ.

"Those who live according to the flesh have their minds set on what the flesh desires; but those who live in accordance with the Spirit have their minds set on what the Spirit desires. The mind governed by the flesh is death, but the mind governed by the Spirit is life and peace."(Romans 8:5-6)

Have Faith and Trust

My Precious One
All is in My hands. You must believe this deeply and hold on to the truth of it and your faith will be made whole. Rest assured that I am in all circumstances and suffering, or not, is a part of My overall plan for your life.

It is impossible for you in your finite humanness to comprehend all that I have planned for you. I will use you and guide you to allow Me, through you, to further My Kingdom here on this earth. The pains you suffer, the crosses you bear, are all a part of My plan to bring glory to the Creator who made the heavens and the earth. The joy will be mine, but as an heir, you too will receive great blessings in abundance for your faithfulness to serve Me and worship and adore Me.

You, my child, are a precious part of My plan. Your joy will be made full even in the midst of your suffering as you come to understand more and more My purposes for your life. Rest assured, everything is going perfectly as planned. Your deep faith and trust in Me will bring to completion all that I know is best for you and for your friends and loved ones that you find on your path in life. Nothing is by chance. All is in order, set and ready to go.

Give Me each new day, knowing that when you relinquish all to Me, it frees Me to work in amazing ways. Seek to see everything through My eyes and My perspective knowing that "all things work together for good for those who love the Lord and are called according to his purpose under heaven" (Romans 8:28). Joy now in knowing this truth. Believe it. Internalize it and it will set you free: free from worry, free from pain, free from insecurity, for I am your security in all things and in all places. I am your Father God and I care for you deeply, beyond questionable measure.

Allow Me to wrap you in My arms, love and comfort you, no matter where you are or what you are experiencing. Today is a new day. A joyful day. Give it to Me and then watch to see how I will move. Watch to see My miracles unfold. Hold onto your faith and trust Me when you are not allowed to see the whole and things don't look so good at the present. Know that it all will be good for you and those other lives you have touched.

———

First Corinthians 13:1-13 is all about LOVE. Father God, I need more love.

Karen Lunde Wiley and her husband, Mike Young

ABOUT THE AUTHOR

Karen Lunde Wiley is a survivor of immense grief and trauma—a woman who walked into victory by claiming God's grace and peace over her life.

After her first husband's untimely death in 1994, Karen—as a single, working mother—raised her daughter and son while teaching elementary school and pouring her heart into helping others, wanting them to understand the fullness of God's healing love for them, just as she had experienced it herself.

In 1997, Karen heard God speak to her, telling her she was the bride of Christ, and that one day she would write a book about it. She sensed God's voice telling her she would be made whole through intimacy with Him, and would be given the opportunity to travel and speak about her experiences. Today, that vision has come to fruition.

After 24 years of not dating, Karen met her current husband, Mike Young. Together, they lead in ministry at their church in Knoxville, Tennessee, and mentor a group of young adults in their home, helping them to discover Jesus Christ as their bridegroom.

Karen graduated from the University of Washington with a BA in Speech Communications, and also holds an MA in

Elementary Education from Tusculum College. She was an educator and teacher for thirty years. She is a mother of two grown children and a grandmother of three.

Karen may be contacted through her website, www.karen-lundewiley.com.

CPSIA information can be obtained
at www.ICGtesting.com
Printed in the USA
BVHW070920120820
586035BV00005B/9